# 125 best
# Indoor Grill
# recipes

# 125 best Indoor Grill recipes

## ILANA SIMON

Robert
ROSE

**For complete cataloguing information, see page 182.**

Disclaimer
The recipes in this book have been carefully tested by our kitchen and our tasters. To the best of our knowledge, they are safe and nutritious for ordinary use and users. For those people with food or other allergies, or who have special food requirements or health issues, please read the suggested contents of each recipe carefully and determine whether or not they may create a problem for you. All recipes are used at the risk of the consumer. Consumers should always consult their indoor grill manufacturer's manual for recommended procedures and cooking times.

We cannot be responsible for any hazards, loss or damage that may occur as a result of any recipe use.

For those with special needs, allergies, requirements or health problems, in the event of any doubt, please contact your medical advisor prior to the use of any recipe.

Design & Production: PageWave Graphics Inc.
Editor: Sue Sumeraj
Photography: Mark T. Shapiro
Food Styling: Kate Bush
Prop Styling: Charlene Erricson
Index: Gillian Watts

Cover image: Lemon-Pepper Fish Fillets (page 138)

We acknowledge the financial support of the Government of Canada through the Book Publishing Industry Development Program (BPIDP) for our publishing activities.

Published by Robert Rose Inc.
120 Eglinton Avenue East, Suite 800, Toronto, Ontario, Canada M4P 1E2
Tel: (416) 322-6552; Fax: (416) 322-6936

Printed in Canada

1 2 3 4 5 6 7 8 9 FP 12 11 10 09 08 07 06 05 04

# Contents

Acknowledgments . . . . . . . . . . . . . . . . . . . . . . . . . . . . . 6

Introduction . . . . . . . . . . . . . . . . . . . . . . . . . . . . . . . 7


Appetizers . . . . . . . . . . . . . . . . . . . . . . . . . . . . . . . 15

Salads and Side Dishes . . . . . . . . . . . . . . . . . . . . . . 35

Sandwiches . . . . . . . . . . . . . . . . . . . . . . . . . . . . . . 51

Burgers . . . . . . . . . . . . . . . . . . . . . . . . . . . . . . . . 67

Main Entrées: Beef . . . . . . . . . . . . . . . . . . . . . . . . . 89

Main Entrées: Chicken and Turkey . . . . . . . . . . . . . . 107

Main Entrées: Fish and Seafood . . . . . . . . . . . . . . . . 133

Main Entrées: Pork, Lamb and Veal . . . . . . . . . . . . . 155

Desserts . . . . . . . . . . . . . . . . . . . . . . . . . . . . . . . . 173


Index . . . . . . . . . . . . . . . . . . . . . . . . . . . . . . . . . . . 183

# Acknowledgments

CREATING THIS COOKBOOK has been a thrilling grilling experience! The indoor grill is an amazing and versatile appliance that helps put dinner on the table quickly and easily. I could not have succeeded without the assistance of my number one taste-testers: my husband, Ari Marantz, and my sons, Jesse and Evan. Thank you for your enduring love and support — as well as important contributions and suggestions to make this cookbook sizzle!

Thank you to my publisher, Bob Dees, whose inspiration and enthusiasm is always appreciated. It's been a pleasure working with you again.

Many people helped bring this cookbook to life. Thanks to the brilliant creative team: editor Sue Sumeraj, an excellent editor with keen good judgment; Kevin Cockburn and Daniella Zanchetta at PageWave Graphics for the exceptional book design and layout; and recipe tester Jennifer MacKenzie for her invaluable input. The fabulous food photography you see throughout the book is at the hands of talented food stylist Kate Bush, props stylist Charlene Erricson and food photographer Mark Shapiro.

I am so fortunate to have friends and family who continually reinforce my cookbook writing efforts and offer endless encouragement. Thank you to my friends Cara Kroft, Robyn Lerner and Brenda Suderman for being there for me throughout this process.

I am grateful to my in-laws, Brenda and Bill Marantz, for all of their support. Cheers, as well, to my dear sisters, Anna-Gail, Sherrill and Debbie, and their families, for their unwavering belief in me (especially to my "416" ears.) Special thanks to my mom and dad, Betty and Monte Simon, for always cheering me on and being the best PR team any cookbook author could want.

# Introduction

EVERYONE LOVES A good barbecue. That smoky, seared flavor derived from barbecuing is synonymous with summer, carefree cuisine and great grilled gastronomy.

Now, there's a new kid on the barbecue block: the electric indoor grill, which lets you enjoy grilling all year round from the comforts of your kitchen. No fuss, no mess, no fat — no brainer!

Indoor grills have taken the North American market by storm, jiving with an increasing penchant for high protein, low-carb meals. They are now widely available at department stores, supermarkets, drugstores and via the Internet. They have become the microwaves of the twenty-first century as the must-have appliance for every household. An estimated 2.5 million indoor grills are sold each year. Indoor grills promise — and deliver — convenience, versatility and uncomplicated cooking. What's not to like about that?

The easy-to-use appliance replicates the outdoor barbecue taste and texture without the worries of singeing your hair, burning the meat, flame flare-ups or any of the other pesky problems associated with outdoor grilling. The result is mouth-watering, grilled, lower-fat fare in mere minutes.

Ideal for any apartment, house or cottage, your portable indoor grill will create healthy and economical meals, usually in less than fifteen minutes. And, as you'll soon discover, it's wonderful, for more than simply cooking burgers and hot dogs! Indoor grilling is a fast and satisfying way to prepare gourmet meals such as pesto chicken and honey dill salmon with Dijon mustard, or to rustle up your favorite comfort foods such as grilled tuna melts and saucy pork chops.

True, the indoor grill is perfect for fast and flavorful family meals on busy weekdays when time is of the essence. You'll come to rely on homemade teriyaki chicken breasts, perfect panini and fast fajitas. You'll rarely be tempted to go the fast-food route when you can so easily prepare your own fast food — from chicken nuggets to maple-glazed pork chops to the ultimate hamburger — on the indoor grill in less time than it takes to order in a pizza.

However, the indoor grill is also suited to entertaining dinner guests. You can skillfully grill succulent pepper steak, lamb kofte, coconut mango chicken or honey orange salmon with thyme. For a cocktail party, whip up bacon-wrapped scallops, spicy shrimp kabobs, tempura vegetables and grilled eggplant baba ghanouj. Brunch or lunch favorites include French toast, grilled cheese and asparagus rolls, Reuben sandwiches, chicken Caesar salad and Thai noodle salad.

Not only can you can create classy, delicious cuisine for family and friends, but you can do it quickly and almost effortlessly. You can marinate meat, poultry, fish or seafood earlier in the day and prepare all of the accompaniments, such as rice pilaf, vegetables and salad, in advance. When your guests arrive, you can grill the "all set to go" appetizers (most are ready in minutes!), enjoy time visiting and then grill the main entrée just before you are ready to sit down to dinner. Entertaining doesn't get much easier than that!

Unlike with a backyard barbecue, there's no need to constantly check, flip and fret about your grill grub or be anxious about running out of propane. No worries, either, about whether the food will be charred on the outside but undercooked on the inside. The uniform heat of the indoor grill results in evenly and thoroughly cooked foods, especially in the covered contact grill, which I highly recommend.

One of the most enticing aspects of the indoor grill is its accessibility. You don't need to be a barbecue authority, or even have outdoor barbecue experience. Anyone can learn to indoor grill, and with the help of *125 Best Indoor Grill Recipes*, you will become hooked on the fabulous fish, the moist boneless, skinless chicken breasts and thighs, the flavorful steaks and burgers. And you will be amazed at the mealtime options open to you, rain or shine, when you can confidently assume grilling duties and count on your handy indoor grill to serve up speedy suppertime solutions.

If you already own an indoor grill, you'll discover a world of possibilities you may never have considered. If you're a novice indoor griller, you will be amazed at what this little appliance can do for your dinner menu.

You will love my innovative twist on typically deep-fried faves such as grilled southern fried chicken, jalapeño poppers and tempura shrimp and vegetables. And my original indoor grill recipes such as chicken and bean burritos, blackened red fish and veal Parmagiana will motivate you to adapt your own favorites to the indoor grill. I have also included a myriad of marinades to season and spice up main entrée meats, poultry and fish. Finally, my selection of creative vegetarian dishes such as portobello mushroom burgers, Asian-flavored grilled tofu and grilled potato pancakes will inspire you. As you become more comfortable taking your indoor grill in new directions, you will discover and enjoy its many capabilities, from aromatic grilled vegetables to awesome grilled fruit.

Prepare to tempt your taste buds, expand your grilling horizons and explore the variety of recipes found in this cookbook. Thanks to *125 Best Indoor Grill Recipes*, you'll never run out of ideas for your indoor grill, and you'll learn it has more potential than you ever imagined.

Enjoy the thrill of the indoor grill!

— Ilana Simon

# Types of Indoor Grills

## Two-sided or contact indoor grills

One of the most popular brands of indoor grills on the market today bears the name of a high-profile sports celebrity. This brand is representative of the new generation of covered or contact indoor grills saturating the market. And for good reason! The two-sided grills feature hinged lids and heat from both the bottom and the top. Contact grills cook twice as fast as the uncovered hibachi-style indoor grills. They come in a variety of sizes and wattages (not to mention colors) to suit your family's needs, and some are equipped with little extras like bun warmers!

Today's contact grills are ideal appliances for healthful cooking. Their non-stick surfaces require little additional fat prior to grilling, and the ridged grill surfaces are slanted downward, causing the fat to drip into a drip tray.

While most indoor grills include only one temperature setting (high), some are equipped with variable temperature controls. For certain dishes — particularly fish — I recommend a medium-high temperature for grilling. If your grill does not feature this option, simply check for doneness at the low end of the range of my recommended grilling time. Also, consult the manufacturer's instructions for suggested grill times on your model of indoor grill. (Times may vary slightly depending on the wattage and size of your indoor grill.)

Higher wattage contact grills (more than 1,200 watts) are more efficient at preheating, cooking large quantities of food at one time and maintaining the desired temperature level. More powerful contact grills also mimic the sought-after crispiness and brown grill marks created by traditional barbecues.

These days, contact grills range in price from about $20 for a two-burger, compact version to up to $150 for an exclusive model that can easily grill four steaks, eight chicken breasts or pork chops, nine large burgers or six to eight fish fillets at one time. In addition to the extra-large grilling surface, the more expensive model should feature variable temperature settings, a timer and a hinged lid to accommodate various thicknesses of foods.

## One-sided or hibachi-style indoor grills

One-sided indoor grills feature open grates for the large grill surface and a removable drip tray located directly beneath the grill to catch juice and fat drippings. It is recommended on some models that a small amount of water be poured into the drip tray to achieve smokeless grilling. Many one-sided indoor grills are also equipped with a second solid griddle surface that can replace the open-grate grill for pancakes and the like.

In general, one-sided indoor grills require cooking times of twice as long as the dual-sided contact grills. All of my recipes may be adapted to the hibachi-style grill by doubling the grilling time (or suggested range of grilling times) and flipping the food at the halfway point. Consult the manufacturer's instructions for the recommended grilling times of specific foods on your model.

One-sided indoor grills do tend to feature variable temperature settings, which facilitate warming and grilling foods such as fish at medium-high, as opposed to high.

# Indoor Grilling vs. Backyard Barbecuing

In addition to fostering year-round grilling opportunities, your indoor grill is also designed to produce a "moveable feast." The portable appliance can easily be set up on any tabletop or countertop in your house, apartment, condo or cottage. You can pack it in your car when you travel to warmer climates for the winter or take it along for no-fuss meal prep at the lake. Some models may also be used outdoors (please check your manufacturer's instructions.)

Because there are no open slats on the contact grill, you don't have to be concerned about vegetables and kabobs falling through the grill openings. And steaks, chicken and fish — to name just a few examples — taste as good, or better, when prepared on your indoor grill rather than on your barbecue. The two-sided contact grill applies heat through the grids directly onto foods, allowing for crystallization of sugars on the outer surfaces of the food. This creates crispy outer surfaces and barbecue-like grill marks.

Indoor grills are also a boon to our nation-wide quest to eat healthy. The non-stick sloped grilling plates allow fat to drip away from food into a stand-alone drip tray positioned at the front of the grill.

A further enticement of indoor grills is the undemanding cleanup. The non-stick surfaces, naturally, are easy to wipe clean. To prevent sticky buildup of sauces or marinades, I recommend lightly spraying your indoor grill with vegetable cooking spray or oil before beginning to grill. Drip pans are dishwasher safe, as are the nylon cooking utensils recommended for use on indoor grills. Once grilling is completed, allow your grill to cool only slightly, then immediately wipe it (while it's still a little warm) with hot soapy water. This will guarantee a painless cleanup every time.

# Indoor Grilling 101

- *Always preheat your indoor grill.* Most indoor grills take a maximum of ten minutes to preheat. Follow manufacturer's directions for best results.

- *Spray it, don't say it.* Before grilling, spray your non-stick grilling surface lightly with vegetable cooking spray or a spray pump filled with olive or vegetable oil. This adds a welcome crispiness to the outer surfaces of foods and helps prevent sauces, coatings and marinades from sticking to the grill surface.

- *Don't be a drip.* Always position your drip tray in its appropriate place. Most of the drip trays are free-standing; some affix to the grill. Either way, if you forget to place your drip tray in front of the sloping grill plates, you may wind up with a puddle of fat on your table or countertop!

- *Be patient.* It takes only minutes to indoor grill. Do not open the contact grill at the halfway point. It is not necessary to flip food, since heat is applied directly on food from both the top and the bottom grill plate. Opening the lid will lower the indoor grill's temperature and affect cooking times.

- *Time is on your side.* A digital timer takes the guesswork away and is ideal for precision indoor grilling. Some indoor grills are equipped with timers. You can also use your microwave timer.

- *Take your food's temperature.* Use a digital thermometer to determine whether your food is cooked through. This is particularly useful for inexperienced indoor grillers. Simply insert the probe into the side of the meat, fish or poultry to test whether the food has reached the recommended internal cooking temperature (see chart, page 14).

- *Do not overcook your food.* Because the contact grill is by far the most popular indoor grill on the market, I have provided cooking times for this type of indoor grill. Remember, heat emanates from the top *and* bottom, cooking foods in about half the time it takes on a backyard barbecue or hibachi-style indoor grill. Establish a new mindset when it comes to indoor grilling, or you will wind up with food that resembles rubber or shoe leather!

- *The nose knows.* Most foods prepared on the indoor grill will not result in unpleasant odors. You may find that fish and seafood are the exception. If possible, open a window or place your indoor grill near an overhead oven range hood to eliminate any unwanted kitchen odors. If you place your indoor grill directly on top of your stove, make sure you have burner covers in place and that all elements are shut off.

- *Turn on/off.* Most grills are equipped with an indicator light that turns on when the grill is plugged in and off once it is turned off. Be sure not to inadvertently leave your indoor grill on.

- *Wash your grill after each use.* This will kill any bacteria that may have been present on raw meat or poultry. Use a nylon scrub brush and hot soapy water. It's best to clean the grill right away, while it is still slightly warm. Never use steel wool on non-stick surfaces.

# The Indoor Grilling Pantry

Isn't it great when you have everything you need right at hand? With these tools and basic ingredients, you'll be ready to whip up a feast on your indoor grill at a moment's notice:

## Tools
- an aerosol can of vegetable cooking spray or a spray pump filled with olive oil or vegetable oil
- bamboo skewers for kabobs
- a brush for marinades and pastes
- a large nylon spatula for removing burgers, sandwiches, quesadillas, fish fillets and chicken pieces
- a three-pronged nylon fork for removing steaks and chops
- nylon tongs for removing hot dogs, vegetables and kebabs
- a nylon scrub brush for removing stubborn sauces from the ridged grill surface

## Dishes
- shallow Pyrex casserole dishes (round and oval) for marinating
- a large shallow bowl for coating
- large serving platters
- medium serving platters

## Main ingredients

- boneless, skinless chicken breasts and chicken thighs
- top sirloin steak
- boneless pork chops
- veal scallops
- lamb chops
- salmon and other fish fillets
- halibut and tuna steaks
- ground beef
- ground chicken and turkey
- tortilla shells
- shredded cheese
- vegetables: onions, garlic, peppers, mushrooms, zucchini, lettuce, tomatoes
- fresh herbs: cilantro and parsley

## Ingredients for marinades and pastes

- soy sauce
- lemons and limes
- fruit juices
- vinegars: white, white wine, balsamic, cider
- honey
- brown sugar
- granulated sugar
- olive oil and vegetable oil
- hot pepper sauce and/or chili sauce
- ketchup
- kosher salt
- freshly ground black pepper
- dried herbs: oregano, basil, hot pepper flakes

# Recommended Internal Cooking Temperature and Approximate Grilling Times

| Food | Internal Temperature | Grilling Time (Approx.) | Grill Temperature |
|---|---|---|---|
| **Beef** | | | |
| Beef steak (3/4-inch to 1-inch/1.5 to 2 cm thick) | 160°F (71°C) medium | 3 to 4 minutes | High |
| Beef steak (3/4-inch to 1-inch/1.5 to 2 cm thick) | 170°F (75°C) well-done | 6 minutes | High |
| Ground beef | 160°F (71°C) | 5 to 7 minutes | High |
| **Chicken/Turkey** | | | |
| Boneless, skinless chicken/turkey thighs | 170°F (75°C) | 5 to 6 minutes | High |
| Boneless, skinless chicken/turkey breasts | 170°F (75°C) | 5 to 6 minutes | High |
| Breaded, boneless, skinless chicken/turkey thighs and breasts | 170°F (75°C) | 6 to 7 minutes | High |
| Ground chicken/turkey | 175°F (80°C) | 6 to 8 minutes | High |
| **Fish and Seafood** | | | |
| Fillets (1/2-inch to 3/4-inch/1 to 1.5 cm thick) | 145°F (63°C) | 4 to 6 minutes | Medium-high |
| Breaded fillets | 145°F (63°C) | 5 to 7 minutes | Medium-high |
| Steaks (3/4-inch to 1-inch/1.5 to 2 cm thick) | 145°F (63°C) | 5 to 6 minutes | Medium-high |
| Shrimp (large) | 145°F (63°C) | 2 minutes | Medium-high |
| Ground or flaked fish | 155°F (68°C) | 7 to 8 minutes | High |
| **Lamb** | | | |
| Lamb chops (bone-in) | 160°F (71°C) | 6 to 8 minutes | High |
| Boneless lamb chops | 160°F (71°C) | 5 to 7 minutes | High |
| Ground lamb | 170°F (75°C) | 7 to 9 minutes | High |
| **Pork** | | | |
| Boneless pork loin chops | 160°F (71°C) medium-well | 5 to 6 minutes | High |
| Boneless pork loin chops | 170°F (75°C) well-done | 8 minutes | High |
| Pork sausage (whole, split) | 170°F (75°C) | 12 minutes | High |
| Ground pork | 160°F (71°C) | 7 to 8 minutes | High |
| **Veal** | | | |
| Veal cutlets, breaded | 160°F (71°C) medium-well | 6 to 8 minutes | High |
| Ground veal | 160°F (71°C) | 6 to 8 minutes | High |

# Appetizers

Grilled Eggplant Baba Ghanouj . . . . . . . . . . . . . . . . . . 16

Crostini with Grilled Eggplant and Chèvre . . . . . . . . . 17

Wild Mushroom Bruschetta . . . . . . . . . . . . . . . . . . . 18

Jalapeño Poppers . . . . . . . . . . . . . . . . . . . . . . . . 19

Mushroom-Filled Beef Rollups . . . . . . . . . . . . . . . . . 20

Beef Rollups with Asparagus and Goat Cheese . . . . . . . 22

Chicken Shish Kabobs . . . . . . . . . . . . . . . . . . . . . 23

Chinese-Style Breaded Veal Nuggets . . . . . . . . . . . . . 24

Bacon-Wrapped Scallops . . . . . . . . . . . . . . . . . . . 25

Crab Cakes with Red Pepper Aïoli . . . . . . . . . . . . . . 26

Chipotle Chili–Spiked Shrimp . . . . . . . . . . . . . . . . . 28

Shrimp Satay . . . . . . . . . . . . . . . . . . . . . . . . . . 29

Tempura Shrimp and Vegetables . . . . . . . . . . . . . . . 30

Spicy Shrimp . . . . . . . . . . . . . . . . . . . . . . . . . . 32

Pea Soup with Grilled Hot Dogs . . . . . . . . . . . . . . . 33

Lentil Soup with Grilled Garlic Sausage . . . . . . . . . . . 34

# Grilled Eggplant Baba Ghanouj

*Most people either love or hate eggplant. If you're a fan, you appreciate its mellow flavor, which combines extremely well with garlic and other seasonings. If you're not, try this recipe out — you may become a convert!*

If your contact grill has more than one temperature setting, set it to high for this recipe.

**Tip**
Take the baba ghanouj up a notch by using roasted garlic. Serve with lavash or pita wedges.

**Make Ahead**
Baba Ghanouj can be prepared up to 2 days in advance.

• Preheat contact grill

| | | |
|---|---|---|
| 1 | eggplant, sliced in ½-inch (1 cm) slices | 1 |
| 2 | cloves garlic | 2 |
| | Juice of ½ lemon | |
| 2 tbsp | tahini | 25 mL |
| 2 tbsp | plain yogurt or sour cream | 25 mL |
| 1 tsp | olive oil | 5 mL |
| ¼ tsp | salt | 1 mL |
| ¼ tsp | freshly ground black pepper | 1 mL |
| 1 tbsp | chopped fresh parsley | 15 mL |

1. Spray eggplant slices using a spray pump filled with olive oil or vegetable oil. Place on grill, close lid and grill for 5 to 6 minutes, or until soft and grill-marked. Let cool.

2. Remove skin and place eggplant in food processor with garlic, lemon juice, tahini, yogurt, olive oil, salt and pepper. Process with on/off pulses just until smooth. Do not over-process. Cover and refrigerate until chilled, for at least 2 hours before serving.

3. Sprinkle with parsley before serving.

**Variation**
Instead of serving as a dip, make wraps by spreading baba ghanouj on a tortilla shell, top with spinach leaves and roll. Wrap rolls tightly in plastic wrap, refrigerate for several hours. Slice on the diagonal in 1-inch (2.5 cm) slices and serve as appetizers.

# Crostini with Grilled Eggplant and Chèvre

*These appetizers make a fabulous focal point for any appetizer tray.*

If your contact grill has more than one temperature setting, set it to high for this recipe.

**Tip**

As is often the case with marinades, it's easiest to brush one side of the eggplant slice, place on grill brushed-side down, and then brush opposite side with remainder of marinade.

**Make Ahead**

Grill eggplant slices up to 1 day in advance. Cover and refrigerate. Assemble crostini just before serving.

• **Preheat contact grill**

| | | |
|---|---|---|
| 2 | cloves garlic, minced | 2 |
| 1 tbsp | olive oil | 15 mL |
| 1 tbsp | balsamic vinegar | 15 mL |
| 1 tsp | dried Italian seasoning | 5 mL |
| 1/2 tsp | kosher salt | 2 mL |
| 1/2 tsp | freshly ground black pepper | 2 mL |
| 1 | eggplant, sliced in 1/4-inch (0.5 cm) slices | 1 |
| 1 | baguette, sliced in 1/2-inch (1 cm) slices | 1 |
| 2 tbsp | chopped fresh basil | 25 mL |
| 4 oz | soft chèvre (goat cheese) | 125 g |

1. In a small bowl, whisk together garlic, olive oil, vinegar, Italian seasoning, salt and pepper.

2. Brush both sides of eggplant slices with oil mixture.

3. Spray both sides of contact grill with vegetable cooking spray or oil. Place eggplant on grill, close lid and grill for 6 minutes, until grill-marked. Set aside.

4. Place baguette slices on grill, close lid and grill for 2 minutes, until lightly toasted.

5. Slice large eggplant slices in half and place each portion on a single slice of baguette. Top with a smear of goat cheese. Sprinkle on chopped basil.

6. Return crostini to grill and carefully hold lid down (not quite touching or cheese will stick) for 2 minutes, or until cheese is melted.

**Variation**

Instead of melting cheese on the grill, place crostini on a baking sheet under the oven broiler for 1 to 2 minutes until cheese is melted.

# Wild Mushroom Bruschetta

*This variation on the traditional tomato-based bruschetta is appealing to mushroom maniacs and is great served with chilled chardonnay.*

If your contact grill has more than one temperature setting, set it to high for this recipe.

## Tip

Use any combination of shiitake, chanterelle or portobello mushrooms.

## Make Ahead

Grill mushrooms and shallots and prepare wild mushroom mixture up to 1 day in advance. Cover and refrigerate. Assemble bruschetta just before serving.

• **Preheat contact grill**

| | | |
|---|---|---|
| 1 lb | wild mushrooms, halved | 500 g |
| 2 | shallots, sliced in sixths (about $1/2$ cup/125 mL) | 2 |
| 1 | baguette, sliced in $1/2$-inch (1 cm) slices | 1 |
| 1 tbsp | olive oil | 15 mL |
| $1/4$ cup | chopped fresh basil | 50 mL |
| $1/2$ tsp | kosher salt | 2 mL |
| $1/2$ tsp | freshly ground black pepper | 2 mL |
| | Freshly grated Parmesan cheese | |

1. Spray both sides of contact grill with vegetable cooking spray or oil. Grill mushrooms and shallots for 3 minutes until softened. Set aside.
2. Brush baguette slices with oil. Place on grill, close lid and grill for 2 minutes, until lightly toasted.
3. Chop mushrooms and shallots finely. Add basil, salt and pepper. Mix well.
4. Spread 2 tbsp (25 mL) mushroom mixture onto each baguette slice and top with a sprinkle of Parmesan.
5. Return baguette slices to grill and carefully hold cover down (not quite touching or cheese will stick) for 2 minutes, or until cheese is melted.

### Variation

Instead of melting cheese on the grill, place bruschetta on a baking sheet under the oven broiler for 1 to 2 minutes until cheese is melted.

# Jalapeño Poppers

*Cream cheese-filled
jalapeño poppers are
nothing if not piquant.
The combination of
the spicy peppers with
the cream cheese is
unbeatable.*

If your contact grill
has more than one
temperature setting,
set it to high for
this recipe.

## Tips

Various hot peppers are
widely available now.
Beware of the red hot
peppers — they are fiery!
There are also some
green, yellow and orange
peppers that pack plenty
of punch. Watch out for
hot varieties such as
habañero, Scotch bonnet
and some poblano chiles.

Use milder peppers
such as Anaheim chiles
if available.

| | | |
|---|---|---|
| 8 oz | jalapeño peppers (about 15 medium, 3 inches/7.5 cm long) | 250 g |
| **Filling** | | |
| 1/3 cup | cream cheese, softened (about 3 oz/90g) | 75 mL |
| 1 tbsp | freshly squeezed lemon juice | 15 mL |
| 1/4 tsp | garlic powder | 1 mL |
| Pinch | onion powder | Pinch |
| Pinch | kosher salt | Pinch |
| Pinch | freshly ground black pepper | Pinch |
| **Coating** | | |
| 1/2 cup | cornmeal | 125 mL |
| 1/4 cup | dry bread crumbs | 50 mL |
| 2 tbsp | freshly grated Parmesan cheese | 25 mL |
| 1 | egg, beaten | 1 |

1. Cut off the top of each pepper. With a sharp knife, carefully remove the seeds and membranes, keeping the pepper intact.
2. *Prepare filling:* In a small bowl, mix together cream cheese, lemon juice, garlic powder, onion powder, salt and pepper.
3. Fill each pepper with cream cheese mixture.
4. *Prepare coating:* In a shallow bowl, stir together cornmeal, breadcrumbs and Parmesan cheese.
5. Dip each pepper in beaten egg and then roll in cornmeal coating. Place peppers on baking sheet. Discard any excess egg and cornmeal mixture. Refrigerate for a minimum of 20 minutes or for up to 1 hour. Meanwhile, preheat contact grill.
6. Spray both sides with vegetable cooking spray or oil. Spray coated peppers using a spray pump filled with olive oil or vegetable oil. Place on grill, close lid and grill for 3 to 4 minutes, or until coating is golden and peppers are softened.

# Mushroom-Filled Beef Rollups

*This recipe's palatable pairing of marinated beef and mushrooms will make you want to "roll" it out for any special occasion.*

If your contact grill has more than one temperature setting, set it to high for this recipe.

**Tip**
Dried mushrooms offer an intense, woody flavor that enhances this dish.

**Make Ahead**
Prepare marinade up to 1 day in advance. Cover and refrigerate.

| | | |
|---|---|---|
| 1/4 cup | packed brown sugar | 50 mL |
| 1/4 cup | soy sauce | 50 mL |
| 1 tbsp | steak sauce | 15 mL |
| 1 tbsp | liquid hickory smoke | 15 mL |
| 1/2 tsp | garlic powder | 2 mL |
| 1/4 tsp | freshly ground black pepper | 1 mL |
| 1 lb | inside round beef roulades, sliced into 24 strips (3- by 1-inch/7.5 by 2.5 cm) | 500 g |

**Filling**

| | | |
|---|---|---|
| 1/2 oz | dried porcini mushrooms | 15 g |
| 1 tsp | olive oil | 5 mL |
| 1 | clove garlic, minced | 1 |
| 2 tbsp | minced shallot | 25 mL |
| 1 tbsp | dry bread crumbs | 15 mL |
| 3 | drops hot pepper sauce | 3 |
| 1 tsp | Worcestershire sauce | 5 mL |
| 1/4 tsp | freshly ground black pepper | 1 mL |

1. In a small bowl, stir together brown sugar, soy sauce, steak sauce, liquid hickory smoke, garlic powder and pepper.

2. Place meat in a shallow dish. Brush marinade over meat, stirring well to ensure both sides are covered. Cover and refrigerate for a minimum of 20 minutes. Meanwhile, preheat contact grill.

**3.** *Prepare filling:* In a small bowl, pour 1 cup (250 mL) boiling water over dried mushrooms. Let stand for 20 minutes or until softened. Drain and squeeze out excess moisture. Chop mushrooms finely. In a nonstick skillet, heat oil over medium heat and sauté garlic and shallot for 2 to 3 minutes, until tender. Add mushrooms. Stir in bread crumbs and season with hot pepper sauce, Worcestershire and ground pepper. Mix well and heat for 1 minute.

**4.** *Assemble rollups:* Spread 1 tbsp (15 mL) of filling onto each slice of marinated beef. Roll up jellyroll-style and secure with a toothpick.

**5.** Spray both sides of contact grill with vegetable cooking spray or oil. Place beef rollups on grill, close lid and grill for 5 to 7 minutes, or until steak is cooked to desired doneness.

### Variation
Use other very thinly sliced beef, such as sirloin, in place of inside round.

# Beef Rollups with Asparagus and Goat Cheese

*These eye-catching, elegant appetizers will enhance any tray of hors d'oeuvres.*

If your contact grill has more than one temperature setting, set it to high for this recipe.

## Tips

Roulades is tenderized, thinly sliced round steak and is sometimes labeled "fast-fry."

Liquid smoke is essential to tenderize this beef.

## Make Ahead

Marinate beef overnight, turning several times to ensure both sides of beef are coated in marinade. The longer you marinate the beef, the more tender the results.

| | | |
|---|---|---:|
| 2 | cloves garlic, minced | 2 |
| 1/4 cup | light soy sauce | 50 mL |
| 2 tbsp | prepared chili sauce | 25 mL |
| 1 tbsp | Worcestershire sauce | 15 mL |
| 1 tbsp | liquid hickory smoke | 15 mL |
| 1/4 tsp | freshly ground black pepper | 1 mL |
| 1 lb | inside round beef roulades, sliced into 24 strips (3- by 1-inch/7.5 by 2.5 cm) | 500 g |
| 2 oz | firm goat cheese, sliced into 24 pieces | 60 g |
| 24 | pickled asparagus spears (tops only) | 24 |

1. In a small bowl, stir together garlic, soy sauce, chili sauce, Worcestershire, hickory smoke and pepper.

2. Place meat in a shallow dish. Brush marinade over meat, stirring well to ensure both sides are covered. Cover and refrigerate for a minimum of 20 minutes. Meanwhile, preheat contact grill.

3. *Prepare rollups:* Place 1 piece of goat cheese on each strip of marinated beef and top with 1 asparagus spear placed across strip so only the tip sticks out. Roll up jellyroll-style and secure with a toothpick.

4. Spray both sides of contact grill with vegetable cooking spray or oil. Place beef rollups on grill, close lid and grill for 5 to 7 minutes, or until steak is cooked to desired doneness.

### Variation
Use fresh steamed asparagus in place of pickled asparagus.

# Chicken Shish Kabobs

*The advantage of shish kabobs is that you can assemble and prepare them ahead of time. For amazing appetizers, simply throw them on the grill once your guests arrive.*

If your contact grill has more than one temperature setting, set it to high for this recipe.

## Tip
A combination of red, orange, green and yellow peppers makes a colorful, scrumptious dish that looks fantastic too.

## Make Ahead
Prepare marinade up to 1 day in advance. Cover and refrigerate.

• **Eighteen 9-inch (23 cm) bamboo skewers**

| | | |
|---|---|---|
| 2 | cloves garlic, minced | 2 |
| 3 tbsp | prepared chili sauce | 45 mL |
| 2 tbsp | cranberry sauce | 25 mL |
| 1½ tsp | prepared horseradish | 7 mL |
| 1½ tsp | cider vinegar | 7 mL |
| 1 tsp | Worcestershire sauce | 5 mL |
| 1 tsp | dried onion flakes | 5 mL |
| ½ tsp | kosher salt | 2 mL |
| ¼ tsp | freshly ground black pepper | 1 mL |
| Pinch | hot pepper flakes | Pinch |
| 4 | boneless, skinless chicken breasts, cut in 1-inch (2.5 cm) chunks | 4 |
| 2 | large bell peppers, different colors, cut in 1-inch (2.5 cm) chunks | 2 |
| 1 cup | whole mushrooms, halved | 250 mL |
| 1 | onion, quartered and separated into thin pieces | 1 |

1. Soak bamboo skewers in hot water for 30 minutes.
2. In a small bowl, whisk together garlic, chili sauce, cranberry sauce, horseradish, cider vinegar, Worcestershire, onion flakes, salt, pepper and hot pepper flakes.
3. Thread chicken pieces onto the skewers alternately with peppers, mushrooms and onions. Place skewers in a single layer in a shallow dish.
4. Brush marinade all over skewers. Cover and refrigerate for a minimum of 20 minutes or for up to 1 hour. Meanwhile, preheat contact grill.
5. Spray both sides of contact grill with vegetable cooking spray or oil. Place chicken skewers on grill, close lid and grill for 5 to 6 minutes, or until chicken is no longer pink inside.

# Chinese-Style Breaded Veal Nuggets

MAKES ABOUT 48 NUGGETS

*Some Chinese restaurants serve dried breaded veal, a deep-fried tidbit. My version features Chinese-flavored breaded veal but is much lighter, and less fatty, thanks to healthful indoor grilling.*

If your contact grill has more than one temperature setting, set it to high for this recipe.

**Tip**

Serve with plum sauce or sweet-and-sour sauce.

**Make Ahead**

Prepare veal nuggets in advance to the end of Step 4. Cover and refrigerate for up to 1 day. Grill as directed in Step 5.

| | | |
|---|---|---|
| 4 | veal cutlets (about 1 lb/500 g) | 4 |
| ³⁄₄ cup | corn flakes crumbs | 175 mL |
| ¹⁄₂ cup | all-purpose flour | 125 mL |
| ¹⁄₂ tsp | Chinese five-spice powder (see tip, page 98) | 2 mL |
| ¹⁄₂ tsp | garlic powder | 2 mL |
| ¹⁄₂ tsp | ground ginger | 2 mL |
| ¹⁄₂ tsp | salt | 2 mL |
| ¹⁄₄ tsp | freshly ground black pepper | 1 mL |
| ¹⁄₄ tsp | hot pepper flakes | 1 mL |
| 1 | egg, beaten | 1 |
| 2 tbsp | milk | 25 mL |

1. Cut each veal cutlet into about twelve 1-inch (2.5 cm) cubes.

2. In a medium bowl, combine corn flakes crumbs, flour, five-spice powder, garlic powder, ginger, salt, pepper and hot pepper flakes. Mix well.

3. In a small bowl, stir together beaten egg and milk.

4. Dip each piece of veal first into egg and then into crumb coating. Place on a rimmed baking sheet. Repeat until all pieces are breaded. Cover and refrigerate for a minimum of 20 minutes. Discard any excess egg and coating mixtures. Meanwhile, preheat contact grill.

5. Spray both sides of contact grill with vegetable cooking spray or oil. Place breaded veal nuggets on grill, close lid and grill for 6 to 8 minutes, or until veal is cooked to desired doneness and coating is golden.

**Variation**

For extra crispiness, spray the veal nuggets directly with spray pump filled with olive oil or vegetable oil before grilling.

# Bacon-Wrapped Scallops

MAKES ABOUT
18 APPETIZERS

*This popular appetizer is a cinch on the grill and results in a resounding two thumbs up.*

If your contact grill has more than one temperature setting, set it to high for this recipe.

## Tips

Make sure you use large sea scallops for this recipe. The smaller bay scallops won't give the same results.

Make your own Cajun Spice Blend. See recipe, page 135.

## Make Ahead

Coat scallops and wrap each scallop in bacon. Place on a baking sheet, cover lightly with waxed paper and refrigerate for up to 1 hour until ready to grill.

• Preheat contact grill

| | | |
|---|---|---|
| ½ cup | cornmeal | 125 mL |
| 1 tbsp | Cajun spice seasoning | 15 mL |
| ½ tsp | freshly ground black pepper | 2 mL |
| 1 lb | jumbo sea scallops | 500 g |
| 1 lb | bacon | 500 g |

1. In a small bowl, combine cornmeal, Cajun spice and pepper.

2. Rinse scallops. Do not dry. Dip one at a time in cornmeal coating. Wrap one slice of bacon around each scallop. Secure with a wooden toothpick. Continue until all scallops are wrapped in bacon.

3. Spray both sides of contact grill with vegetable cooking spray or oil. Place scallops on grill, close lid and grill for 5 minutes, or until scallops are firm and opaque and bacon is crisp.

### Variation
In place of the Cajun spice, use dried Italian seasoning.

# Crab Cakes with Red Pepper Aïoli

**MAKES ABOUT 16 CRAB CAKES**

*Mini crab cakes make an awesome appetizer, especially when paired with fiery red pepper aïoli.*

If your contact grill has more than one temperature setting, set it to high for this recipe.

| | | |
|---|---|---|
| 2 | cans crabmeat (each 6 oz/175 g), drained | 2 |
| 1 | clove garlic, minced | 1 |
| 1 | green onion, minced | 1 |
| 1/3 cup | dry bread crumbs | 75 mL |
| 1/3 cup | chopped green bell pepper | 75 mL |
| 1/4 cup | mayonnaise | 50 mL |
| 2 tbsp | chopped fresh parsley | 25 mL |
| 1 tbsp | freshly squeezed lemon juice | 15 mL |
| 3/4 tsp | seasoned salt | 4 mL |
| 1/2 tsp | freshly ground black pepper | 2 mL |
| 1 tbsp | milk | 15 mL |
| | Red Pepper Aïoli (see recipe, opposite) | |

1. In a medium bowl, combine crabmeat, garlic, green onion, bread crumbs, green pepper, mayonnaise, parsley, lemon juice, seasoned salt and pepper. Mix well. Gradually stir in milk.

2. With moistened hands, form mini crab cakes, about 1½ inch (4 cm) in diameter. Place on a baking sheet and refrigerate for 20 minutes. Meanwhile, preheat contact grill.

3. Spray both sides of contact grill with vegetable cooking spray or oil. Also spray both sides of crab cakes using a spray pump filled with olive oil or vegetable oil. Place crab cakes on grill, close lid and grill for 7 to 8 minutes, or until crab cakes are crisp on the outside and heated through. Serve with Red Pepper Aïoli.

**Variation**
Use 12 oz (375 g) cooked fresh or frozen lump crab in place of canned crab.

**Tips**
Use light mayonnaise to lower the fat content.

Seasoned salt is, as its name suggests, table salt seasoned with spices and herbs.

**Make Ahead**
Prepare and grill crab cakes up to 1 day in advance. Cover and refrigerate. Just before serving, heat in a 350°F (180°C) oven for 20 minutes, or until heated through.

# Red Pepper Aïoli

If your contact grill
has more than one
temperature setting,
set it to high for
this recipe.

**Tip**
You can also serve
Red Pepper Aïoli with
Tempura Shrimp and
Vegetables (see page 30).

• **Preheat contact grill**

| | | |
|---|---|---|
| 1 | red bell pepper, halved | 1 |
| 1 | clove garlic | 1 |
| 2 tbsp | fresh parsley | 25 mL |
| 4 | drops chipotle-flavored hot pepper sauce | 4 |
| 1 tbsp | olive oil | 15 mL |
| 1 tsp | freshly squeezed lemon juice | 5 mL |
| ¼ tsp | kosher salt | 1 mL |
| ¼ tsp | freshly ground black pepper | 1 mL |

**1.** Spray red pepper halves all over with olive oil. Place on grill, close lid and grill for 4 minutes or until charred. Place in covered bowl or paper bag and let cool. Peel off skins.

**2.** In food processor, or using hand blender, chop pepper. Add garlic and parsley and process until puréed.

**3.** Add hot pepper sauce, olive oil, lemon juice, salt and pepper to red pepper mixture. Purée until smooth. Transfer to a serving bowl, cover and refrigerate for a minimum of 20 minutes or for up to 2 days. Serve at room temperature.

# Chipotle Chili–Spiked Shrimp

**MAKES 12
SKEWERS (ABOUT
40 SHRIMP)**

*Chipotle chilies in
adobo sauce liven up
this palate-pleasing
hors d'oeuvre.*

If your contact grill
has more than one
temperature setting,
set it to medium-
high for this recipe.

**Tip**

Avoid overcooking
shrimp to prevent them
from becoming tough
and rubbery.

**Make Ahead**

Prepare marinade up to
1 day in advance. Cover
and refrigerate.

- Preheat contact grill
- Twelve 9-inch (23 cm) bamboo skewers

| | | |
|---|---|---|
| 4 | cloves garlic | 4 |
| 1/2 cup | dry red wine | 125 mL |
| 1/4 cup | chopped fresh cilantro | 50 mL |
| 1/4 cup | freshly squeezed lime juice | 50 mL |
| 2 tbsp | olive oil | 25 mL |
| 2 | canned chipotle chili in adobo sauce, minced | 2 |
| 1/2 tsp | kosher salt | 2 mL |
| 1/2 tsp | freshly ground black pepper | 2 mL |
| 2 lb | jumbo shrimp, peeled and deveined | 1 kg |

1. Soak bamboo skewers in hot water for 30 minutes.

2. In food processor, process together garlic, wine, cilantro, lime juice, olive oil, chili in sauce, salt and pepper to form a paste.

3. Thread shrimp loosely onto bamboo skewers, 3 to 4 shrimp per skewer, leaving space at each end. Brush paste over shrimp, covering both sides. Cover and refrigerate for a minimum of 20 minutes or for up to 1 hour.

4. Spray both sides of contact grill with vegetable cooking spray or oil. Place shrimp skewers on grill, close lid and grill for 2 minutes, or until shrimp are pink and opaque.

**Variation**

Instead of threading shrimp on skewers, place directly on grill. Check after 2 minutes.

# Shrimp Satay

*These spicy shrimp satays will be the stars of your appetizer tray.*

If your contact grill has more than one temperature setting, set it to medium-high for this recipe.

## Tip

Use natural smooth peanut butter for best results. If using processed peanut butter, reduce the amount of honey by half.

## Make Ahead

Prepare peanut sauce up to 2 days in advance. Cover and refrigerate.

- Preheat contact grill
- Twelve 9-inch (23 cm) bamboo skewers

| | | |
|---|---|---|
| 4 | cloves garlic | 4 |
| $1/4$ cup | peanut butter | 50 mL |
| 2 tbsp | soy sauce | 25 mL |
| 2 tbsp | sesame oil | 25 mL |
| 2 tbsp | seasoned rice vinegar | 25 mL |
| 2 tbsp | minced gingerroot | 25 mL |
| 2 tbsp | liquid honey | 25 mL |
| 2 lb | jumbo shrimp, peeled and deveined | 1 kg |

1. Soak bamboo skewers in hot water for 30 minutes.

2. In food processor, mince garlic. Add peanut butter, soy sauce, sesame oil, rice vinegar, gingerroot and honey, and process until smooth.

3. Thread shrimp loosely onto bamboo skewers, 3 to 4 shrimp per skewer, leaving space at each end. Brush sauce over shrimp, covering both sides. Cover and refrigerate for a minimum of 20 minutes or for up to 1 hour.

4. Spray both sides of contact grill with vegetable cooking spray or oil. Place shrimp skewers on grill, close lid and grill for 2 minutes, or until shrimp are pink and opaque.

### Variation
Use 1 lb (500 g) of boneless, skinless chicken breasts, cut in 1-inch (2.5 cm) chunks, in place of shrimp. Increase grilling time to 6 minutes.

# Tempura Shrimp and Vegetables

*This tempura recipe, supplied by recipe tester Cheryl Warkentin, works amazingly well on the indoor grill. And guess what? Unlike the usual tempura deep-fry method, very little oil is required!*

If your contact grill has more than one temperature setting, set it to high for this recipe.

## Tip

Serve with choice of seafood sauce, peanut sauce and light soy sauce for dipping.

## Make Ahead

Prepare tempura batter and coat vegetables and seafood in batter. Refrigerate for up to 2 hours before grilling.

- Preheat contact grill
- Preheat oven to 325°F (160°C)

| | | |
|---|---|---|
| 2 cups | cauliflower florets (about 8 oz/250 g) | 500 mL |
| 2 cups | broccoli florets (about 8 oz/250 g) | 500 mL |
| 1 lb | jumbo shrimp, peeled and deveined | 500 g |
| **Batter** | | |
| 2 | eggs | 2 |
| 1 cup | all-purpose flour | 250 mL |
| 3 tbsp | melted butter | 45 mL |
| $\frac{1}{2}$ tsp | kosher salt | 2 mL |
| $\frac{1}{4}$ tsp | freshly ground black pepper | 1 mL |
| 6 tbsp | cold water | 90 mL |

1. *Prepare batter:* In electric mixer bowl, blend eggs, flour, butter, salt and pepper. Mix well.

2. With mixer running, pour in cold water and blend until smooth. Let batter stand at room temperature.

3. Blanch broccoli and cauliflower florets in boiling water for about 3 minutes, or until just softened. Drain and rinse with cold water.

**4.** Dip each floret in tempura batter and place on a baking sheet. Continue until all vegetables are coated in batter. For best results, chill for a minimum of 20 minutes before grilling.

**5.** Dip each shrimp in batter and place on a separate baking sheet. Continue until all shrimp are coated in batter. For best results, chill for a minimum of 20 minutes before grilling. Discard any excess batter.

**6.** Spray both sides of contact grill with vegetable cooking spray or oil. Place vegetables on grill, close lid and grill for 4 minutes, or until batter is golden. Remove and keep warm in preheated oven.

**7.** Place shrimp on grill, close lid and grill for 3 to 4 minutes, or until batter is golden and shrimp are pink and opaque. Serve immediately.

**Variation**
Use other blanched vegetables or your favorite seafood in place of large shrimp.

# Spicy Shrimp

*Shrimp grill quickly on the dual contact indoor grill — perfect for a zesty appetizer, or you can serve these shrimp over pasta for a delectable main entrée.*

If your contact grill has more than one temperature setting, set it to medium-high for this recipe.

## Tip
Look for shrimp in the frozen section for better buys.

## Make Ahead
Prepare garlic mixture up to 1 day in advance. Cover and refrigerate.

- Preheat contact grill
- Twelve 9-inch (23 cm) bamboo skewers

| | | |
|---|---|---|
| 4 | cloves garlic | 4 |
| 1/2 cup | fresh cilantro | 125 mL |
| 6 tbsp | freshly squeezed lime juice | 90 mL |
| 2 tbsp | chopped fresh oregano | 25 mL |
| 2 tsp | hot pepper sauce | 10 mL |
| 1/2 tsp | ground cumin | 2 mL |
| 1/2 tsp | kosher salt | 2 mL |
| 1/2 tsp | freshly ground black pepper | 2 mL |
| 2 lb | jumbo shrimp, peeled and deveined | 1 kg |

1. Soak bamboo skewers in hot water for 30 minutes.

2. In food processor, process together garlic, cilantro, lime juice, oregano, hot pepper sauce, cumin, salt and pepper to form a paste.

3. Thread shrimp loosely onto bamboo skewers, 3 to 4 shrimp per skewer, leaving space at each end. Brush paste over shrimp, covering both sides. Cover and refrigerate for a minimum of 20 minutes or for up to 1 hour.

4. Spray both sides of contact grill with vegetable cooking spray or oil. Place shrimp skewers on grill, close lid and grill for 2 minutes, or until shrimp are pink and opaque.

### Variation
Use 1 tsp (5 mL) chipotle-flavored hot pepper sauce for a smokier version.

Crab Cakes with
Red Pepper Aïoli (page 26)

# Pea Soup with Grilled Hot Dogs

*This recipe was inspired by the fabulous comfort of homemade pea soup made by my mom, Betty Simon. The hot dogs impart a scrumptious smoky flavor.*

If your contact grill has more than one temperature setting, set it to high for this recipe.

**Tip**

Split peas do not have to soak in advance of cooking like other peas.

- Preheat contact grill

| | | |
|---|---|---|
| 1 tbsp | olive oil | 15 mL |
| 2 | cloves garlic, minced | 2 |
| 1 | onion, chopped | 1 |
| 3 | carrots, sliced in rounds | 3 |
| 2 | stalks celery, diced | 2 |
| 8 cups | beef stock | 2 L |
| 1 1/3 cups | dried split green peas, rinsed and drained | 325 mL |
| 1 1/2 tsp | chopped fresh thyme (or 1/2 tsp/2 mL dried) | 7 mL |
| 1/4 tsp | kosher salt | 1 mL |
| 1/4 tsp | freshly ground black pepper | 1 mL |
| 8 oz | all-beef hot dogs | 250 g |

1. In Dutch oven, heat oil over medium heat. Sauté garlic and onion for 3 minutes or until softened. Add carrots and celery. Sauté another 5 minutes until softened. Add stock and peas, thyme, salt and pepper. Bring to a boil over high heat. Reduce heat to medium and cook, covered, for 30 minutes.

2. Meanwhile, place hot dogs on grill, close lid and grill for 5 to 6 minutes, or until hot dogs begin to split. Let cool.

3. Slice hot dogs into 1-inch (2.5 cm) chunks. Add to soup. Cook, covered, for 15 minutes. Remove lid and cook for 15 minutes longer or until soup is thickened.

**Variation**

Use smokies in place of hot dogs.

Shrimp Satay (page 29)

# Lentil Soup with Grilled Garlic Sausage

*Garlic sausage is prevalent on the prairies and gives punch to this winter soup recipe.*

If your contact grill has more than one temperature setting, set it to high for this recipe.

**Tip**

Garlic sausage, also called Polish sausage, is coarse, pre-cooked sausage usually sold in a U or a half-U shape in the deli section, alongside other cold cuts. Grilling garlic sausage brings out its spiciness.

| | | |
|---|---|---|
| 1½ tsp | olive oil | 7 mL |
| 1 | clove garlic, minced | 1 |
| 1 | onion, chopped | 1 |
| 2 | carrots, sliced in rounds | 2 |
| 1 | parsnip, peeled and sliced in rounds | 1 |
| 2 | stalks celery and leaves, diced, divided | 2 |
| 2 | bay leaves | 2 |
| 10 cups | beef stock | 2.5 L |
| 1½ cups | dried small green lentils, rinsed and drained | 375 mL |
| ½ tsp | freshly ground black pepper | 2 mL |
| ¼ tsp | kosher salt | 1 mL |
| 2 tbsp | chopped fresh parsley | 25 mL |
| 8 oz | garlic sausage, sliced in ½-inch (1 cm) thick rounds | 250 g |

1. In a Dutch oven, heat oil over medium heat. Sauté garlic and onion for 3 minutes, or until softened. Add carrots, parsnip and celery stalks. Sauté for another 5 minutes, until softened. Add bay leaves, stock, lentils, celery leaves, pepper and salt and bring to a boil over high heat. Reduce heat to medium and cook, covered, for 1 hour, or until lentils are softened. Meanwhile, preheat contact grill.

2. Place the sausage slices on contact grill, close lid and grill for 5 to 6 minutes, or until grill-marked. Let cool, then halve each slice crosswise.

3. Add sausage pieces to soup. Cook uncovered for 20 to 30 minutes longer, stirring occasionally, until soup is thickened.

**Variation**
Use smokies in place of garlic sausage.

# Salads and Side Dishes

Asian Steak Noodle Salad . . . . . . . . . . . . . . . . . . . . . . . . 36

Chicken Caesar Salad . . . . . . . . . . . . . . . . . . . . . . . . . . 38

Tex-Mex Pasta Salad . . . . . . . . . . . . . . . . . . . . . . . . . . 40

Italian Vegetable and Orzo Salad . . . . . . . . . . . . . . . . . 42

Thai Chicken Noodle Salad . . . . . . . . . . . . . . . . . . . . . 44

Grilled Asparagus . . . . . . . . . . . . . . . . . . . . . . . . . . . . . 46

Grilled Tofu. . . . . . . . . . . . . . . . . . . . . . . . . . . . . . . . . . 47

Grilled Vegetables. . . . . . . . . . . . . . . . . . . . . . . . . . . . . 48

Low-Fat Potato Pancakes . . . . . . . . . . . . . . . . . . . . . . . 50

# Asian Steak Noodle Salad

SERVES 4

*This versatile, aromatic salad is excellent as a light lunch, a starter or a side dish for an Oriental-themed meal.*

If your contact grill has more than one temperature setting, set it to high for this recipe.

## Tips

Feel free to add fresh bean sprouts to this salad.

Tamari, like soy sauce, is made from soybeans, but it offers a milder flavor than soy sauce.

Rice stick noodles do not have to be boiled like regular pasta. They simply require reconstituting in hot water. They are very light and blend well with Asian dressings, bringing out the sweet/sour/hot combination of flavors.

## Make Ahead

Prepare marinade up to 1 day in advance. Cover and refrigerate.

| | | |
|---|---|---|
| 2 | cloves garlic, minced | 2 |
| ¼ cup | tamari | 50 mL |
| 1 tbsp | cider vinegar | 15 mL |
| 1 tsp | ground coriander | 5 mL |
| ½ tsp | hot pepper flakes | 2 mL |
| 1 lb | strip loin beef steak | 500 g |
| 6 oz | Thai rice stick noodles | 175 g |
| ½ | onion, quartered | ½ |
| ½ | red bell pepper, cut in strips | ½ |
| ½ | green bell pepper, cut in strips | ½ |
| 1 | small portobello mushroom, sliced | 1 |
| ½ cup | trimmed snow peas | 125 mL |
| 3 tbsp | chopped roasted peanuts | 45 mL |
| ¼ cup | chopped fresh cilantro | 50 mL |

### Dressing

| | | |
|---|---|---|
| 1 | clove garlic, minced | 1 |
| 3 tbsp | light soy sauce | 45 mL |
| 1 tbsp | rice vinegar | 15 mL |
| 1½ tsp | freshly squeezed lime juice | 7 mL |
| 1 tsp | granulated sugar | 5 mL |
| ½ tsp | sesame oil | 2 mL |
| Pinch | hot pepper flakes | Pinch |

1. In a small bowl, whisk together garlic, tamari, cider vinegar, coriander and hot pepper flakes.

2. Place steak in a shallow dish. Pour marinade over steak, flipping once or twice to coat well. Cover and refrigerate for a minimum of 20 minutes or for up to 1 day.

3. Soak rice stick noodles in hot water for 20 minutes, or until tender. Drain and set aside in a large bowl. Let cool. Meanwhile, preheat contact grill.

**4.** Spray both sides of contact grill with vegetable cooking spray or oil. Separate onion into layers. Place on grill, close lid and grill for 4 to 6 minutes. Add to the bowl with the noodles.

**5.** Lightly spray red and green peppers using a spray pump filled with olive oil or vegetable oil. Place on grill, close lid and grill for 4 minutes. Add to the bowl with the noodles.

**6.** Lightly spray mushroom slices and pea pods with olive oil or vegetable oil. Place on grill, close lid and grill pea pods for 2 minutes and mushrooms for 3 minutes. Add to bowl.

**7.** Place marinated steak on grill, close lid and grill for 3 to 6 minutes, or until steak reaches an internal temperature of 160°F (71°C) for medium or until desired doneness. Cool slightly and slice across the grain in 1-inch (2.5 cm) pieces.

**8.** *Prepare dressing:* Whisk together garlic, soy sauce, vinegar, lime juice, sugar, sesame oil and hot pepper flakes.

**9.** Pour dressing over noodles and vegetables. Add steak. Sprinkle in peanuts and cilantro. Mix well and serve.

### Variation

Use 4 boneless, skinless chicken breasts in place of steak. Grill chicken breasts on high for 6 minutes, or until chicken is no longer pink inside and reaches an internal temperature of 170°F (75°C).

# Chicken Caesar Salad

*What is purportedly the most popular bistro menu item can be yours for the making, thanks to this delicious recipe for grilled chicken Caesar salad. Don't be shy with the garlic — it's good for you! This salad is excellent for lunch or as a light weekday dinner.*

If your contact grill has more than one temperature setting, set it to high for this recipe.

**Tip**

Salty canned anchovies are essential for an authentic Caesar salad. If you simply can't see your way to eating anchovies, you may substitute fried and chopped bacon instead for a less authentic — but still delicious — Caesar salad.

**Make Ahead**

Prepare the salad dressing up to 2 days in advance. Cover and refrigerate.

| | | |
|---|---|---|
| ⅔ cup | dry bread crumbs | 150 mL |
| 1 tsp | dried parsley flakes | 5 mL |
| 1 tsp | seasoned salt (see tip, page 26) | 5 mL |
| ¾ tsp | garlic powder | 4 mL |
| ½ tsp | freshly ground black pepper | 2 mL |
| 1 lb | boneless, skinless chicken breast, sliced in 1-inch (2.5 cm) thick strips | 500 g |
| 1 | egg, beaten | 1 |
| 1 | large head Romaine lettuce, torn, washed and dried (about 8 cups/2 L) | 1 |
| 1 cup | Caesar salad croutons | 250 mL |
| ¼ cup | freshly grated Parmesan cheese | 50 mL |

**Dressing**

| | | |
|---|---|---|
| 3 | cloves garlic | 3 |
| 1 | can (2 oz/56 g) anchovies, drained and dried | 1 |
| ¼ cup | olive oil | 50 mL |
| ¼ cup | vegetable oil | 50 mL |
| 2 tbsp | freshly squeezed lemon juice | 25 mL |
| 2 tbsp | red wine vinegar | 25 mL |
| 1 tbsp | Worcestershire sauce | 15 mL |
| 1 tsp | dry mustard powder | 5 mL |
| | Kosher salt and freshly ground pepper to taste | |

1. In a medium bowl, combine bread crumbs, parsley, seasoned salt, garlic powder and pepper. Mix well.

2. Dip chicken strips, one at a time, in beaten egg, then roll in seasoned bread crumbs until completely covered. Place on a plate. Cover and refrigerate for a minimum of 20 minutes or for up to 1 hour. Discard any excess egg and crumb mixture. Meanwhile, preheat contact grill.

3. *Prepare dressing:* In a food processor, mince garlic. Add anchovies and process with on/off pulses until minced. Add olive and vegetable oils, lemon juice,

vinegar, Worcestershire, dry mustard and salt and pepper to taste and process until smooth.

4. Spray both sides of contact grill with vegetable cooking spray or oil. Place breaded chicken strips on grill, close lid and grill for 6 to 7 minutes, or until coating is crispy and chicken is no longer pink inside.

5. Place Romaine lettuce in a large bowl. Pour in dressing and mix well. Add croutons and Parmesan cheese, tossing to combine. Add chicken to salad, toss well and serve.

**Variation**
Substitute the same amount of cornmeal for the bread crumbs.

# Homemade Croutons

**MAKES ABOUT 8 CUPS (2 L)**

- **Preheat oven to 350°F (180°C)**
- **Cookie sheet**

| | | |
|---|---|---|
| 3 to 4 tbsp | olive oil | 45 to 50 mL |
| 1¼ tsp | garlic powder | 6 mL |
| 1¼ tsp | dried parsley flakes | 6 mL |
| 1 tsp | paprika | 5 mL |
| ¼ tsp | kosher salt | 1 mL |
| ¼ tsp | freshly ground black pepper | 1 mL |
| ½ | loaf day-old bread (French, sourdough or pumpernickel) cut into ½-inch (1 cm) cubes | ½ |

1. Whisk together olive oil, garlic powder, parsley, paprika, salt and pepper.

2. Lay bread cubes on cookie sheet. Brush with olive oil mixture, making sure to coat evenly.

3. Bake in preheated oven for 30 minutes, turning every 10 minutes, until browned.

# Tex-Mex Pasta Salad

*This fiber-friendly steak and pasta salad is unique in taste and texture and makes a vibrant statement.*

If your contact grill has more than one temperature setting, set it to high for this recipe.

## Tip
For an even more colorful dish, use multi-colored rotini for this salad.

## Make Ahead
Cut up vegetables and prepare dressing and marinade up to 1 day in advance. Cover and refrigerate.

| | | |
|---|---|---|
| 2 | cloves garlic, minced | 2 |
| ¼ cup | freshly squeezed lime juice | 50 mL |
| 1 tbsp | ground cumin | 15 mL |
| 2 tsp | dried onion flakes | 10 mL |
| 2 tsp | dried oregano | 10 mL |
| ½ tsp | cayenne pepper | 2 mL |
| ½ tsp | kosher salt | 2 mL |
| Pinch | freshly ground black pepper | Pinch |
| 1 lb | top sirloin beef steak | 500 g |
| 12 oz | rotini pasta | 375 g |
| 1 | red onion, quartered | 1 |
| 1 | red bell pepper, cut into 1-inch (2.5 cm) chunks | 1 |
| 1 | green bell pepper, cut into 1-inch (2.5 cm) chunks | 1 |
| 1 | can (19 oz/540 mL) black beans, drained and rinsed | 1 |
| ½ cup | salsa | 125 mL |
| ½ cup | chopped fresh cilantro | 125 mL |

### Dressing

| | | |
|---|---|---|
| 2 | clove garlic, minced | 2 |
| 3 tbsp | olive oil | 45 mL |
| 1 tbsp | cider vinegar | 15 mL |
| 2 tsp | cumin seeds | 10 mL |
| ½ tsp | kosher salt | 2 mL |
| ½ tsp | freshly ground black pepper | 2 mL |

1. In a small bowl, whisk together garlic, lime juice, cumin, onion flakes, oregano, cayenne, salt and pepper.
2. Place steak in a shallow dish. Pour marinade over steak, flipping once or twice to coat well. Cover and refrigerate for a minimum of 20 minutes or for up to 1 day. Meanwhile, preheat contact grill.

**3.** Cook rotini in boiling salted water for 8 minutes, or until al dente. Drain and cool under cold running water. Place in a large bowl.

**4.** Spray both sides of contact grill with vegetable cooking spray or oil. Separate onion into layers. Place on grill, close lid and grill for 4 to 6 minutes. Add to the rotini.

**5.** Lightly spray red and green peppers using a spray pump filled with olive oil or vegetable oil. Place on grill, close lid and grill for 4 minutes. Add to the rotini.

**6.** Place marinated steak on grill, close lid and grill for 3 to 6 minutes, or until steak reaches an internal temperature of 160°F (71°C) for medium or until desired doneness. Cool slightly and slice across the grain in 1-inch (2.5 cm) pieces. Add to the rotini, along with black beans and salsa.

**7.** *Prepare dressing:* In a small bowl, whisk together garlic, olive oil, cider vinegar, cumin, salt and pepper.

**8.** Stir dressing into pasta salad, mixing well. Sprinkle with cilantro. Toss well to combine.

### Variations

Add about 12 to 18 green olives with pimiento to salad.

Use 4 boneless, skinless chicken breasts in place of steak. Grill chicken breasts on high for 5 to 6 minutes, or until chicken is no longer pink inside and reaches an internal temperature of 170°F (75°C).

Omit black beans if desired.

# Italian Vegetable and Orzo Salad

*Enjoy this burst of summer any time of year thanks to the indoor grill. The artichokes offer a delightful taste and texture and mingle well with the grilled vegetables and orzo.*

If your contact grill has more than one temperature setting, set it to high for this recipe.

**Tip**
This recipe can be halved.

| | | |
|---|---|---|
| 1/2 | red onion, quartered | 1/2 |
| 1 | red bell pepper, cut into 1-inch (2.5 cm) chunks | 1 |
| 1 | green bell pepper, cut into 1-inch (2.5 cm) chunks | 1 |
| 1 cup | mushrooms, halved | 250 mL |
| 2 cups | orzo pasta | 500 mL |
| 1/2 cup | drained and chopped marinated artichokes | 125 mL |
| 4 oz | feta cheese, crumbled | 125 g |

**Dressing**

| | | |
|---|---|---|
| 1 | clove garlic, minced | 1 |
| 3 tbsp | olive oil | 45 mL |
| 2 tbsp | white wine vinegar | 25 mL |
| 2 tbsp | chopped fresh oregano (or 2 tsp/10 mL dried) | 25 mL |
| 2 tbsp | chopped fresh basil (or 2 tsp/10 mL dried) | 25 mL |
| 1 tbsp | chopped fresh mint (or 1 tsp/5 mL dried) | 15 mL |
| 1/2 tsp | kosher salt | 2 mL |
| 1/2 tsp | freshly ground black pepper | 2 mL |

1. *Prepare dressing:* In a small bowl, whisk together garlic, olive oil, vinegar, oregano, basil, mint, salt and pepper.
2. Separate onion into layers. Place in a shallow dish. Brush often with 2 tsp (10 mL) dressing. Toss to coat.
3. Place red and green peppers in shallow dish. Lightly brush with another 2 tsp (10 mL) dressing. Toss to coat.

4. Place mushrooms in a third shallow dish. Brush with 2 tsp (10 mL) dressing. Toss to coat.

5. Marinate all vegetables at room temperature for a minimum of 20 minutes or for up to 2 hours. Meanwhile, preheat contact grill.

6. Cook orzo in boiling salted water for 8 minutes, or until tender. Drain, cool under cold running water and set aside in a large bowl.

7. Spray both sides of contact grill with vegetable cooking spray or oil. Place onions on grill, close lid and grill for 4 to 6 minutes. Return to shallow dish, cover and keep warm.

8. Place red and green peppers on grill, close lid and grill for 4 minutes. Return to shallow dish, cover and keep warm.

9. Place mushrooms on grill, close lid and grill for 3 minutes.

10. Add grilled onions, peppers and mushrooms, artichokes and crumbled feta to orzo. Drizzle remaining dressing over salad. Toss well to combine.

### Variation
Add 12 to 18 pitted black olives to salad.

# Thai Chicken Noodle Salad

*This salad can work as either a brilliant lunch or a fabulous side salad the next time you entertain.*

If your contact grill has more than one temperature setting, set it to high for this recipe.

## Tips

As with any salad, feel free to be creative based on personal preference and what you have on hand.

Use 2 cups (500 mL) packaged fresh coleslaw mixture in place of shredded cabbage and grated carrot, and 2 cups (500 mL) pre-washed, packaged fresh spinach to speed up the preparation.

Fresh herbs provide uncomparable flavor and aroma to this salad. Feel free to add more fresh cilantro and basil, but beware of fresh mint — it can be overpowering.

| | | |
|---|---|---|
| 2 | cloves garlic, minced | 2 |
| 2 tbsp | tamari | 50 mL |
| 1 tbsp | olive oil | 15 mL |
| 1 tbsp | chopped fresh basil | 15 mL |
| 1 tsp | chopped fresh mint | 5 mL |
| 1 tsp | rice vinegar | 5 mL |
| 4 | boneless, skinless chicken breasts (totaling about 1 lb/500 g) | 4 |
| 6 oz | rice vermicelli noodles | 175 g |
| **Salad** | | |
| 1 cup | bean sprouts (about 6 oz/175 g) | 250 mL |
| 2 | green onions, minced | 2 |
| 2 cups | chopped fresh spinach | 500 mL |
| 2 cups | finely shredded Chinese cabbage | 500 mL |
| 1 | carrot, peeled and grated | 1 |
| 2 cups | thinly sliced mixed (red, yellow and green) bell peppers | 500 mL |
| 1 cup | sugar snap peas, trimmed | 250 mL |
| 1/2 cup | chopped fresh cilantro | 125 mL |
| 1/3 cup | chopped fresh basil | 75 mL |
| 1/4 cup | chopped fresh mint | 50 mL |
| **Dressing** | | |
| 1 | clove garlic, minced | 1 |
| 2 tbsp | freshly squeezed lime juice | 25 mL |
| 1 1/2 tbsp | tamari | 22 mL |
| 1 1/2 tbsp | sesame oil | 22 mL |
| 1 tbsp | minced gingerroot | 15 mL |
| 1 tbsp | rice vinegar | 15 mL |
| 1 tsp | granulated sugar | 5 mL |
| 1/4 tsp | hot pepper flakes | 1 mL |

**1.** In a small bowl, whisk together garlic, tamari, olive oil, basil, mint and rice vinegar.

2. Place chicken in a shallow dish. Pour marinade over chicken, flipping once or twice to coat well. Cover and refrigerate for a minimum of 20 minutes. Meanwhile, preheat contact grill.

3. Cook vermicelli noodles in boiling salted water for 9 minutes, or until al dente. Drain, cool under cold running water and place in a large bowl.

4. Spray both sides of contact grill with vegetable cooking spray or oil. Place marinated chicken breasts on grill, close lid and grill for 5 to 6 minutes, or until chicken is no longer pink inside and reaches an internal temperature of 170°F (75°C).

5. *Assemble salad:* Once chicken is grilled, slice into strips. Add to vermicelli, along with bean sprouts, green onions, spinach, cabbage, carrot, bell peppers, snap peas, cilantro, basil and mint. Mix well.

6. *Prepare dressing:* Whisk together garlic, lime juice, tamari, sesame oil, gingerroot, vinegar, sugar and hot pepper flakes. Pour over salad, mix well and serve.

**Variation**
Use 1 lb (500 g) top sirloin steak in place of chicken breasts. Grill on high for 3 to 6 minutes or until steak reaches an internal temperature of 160°F (71°C) for medium or until desired doneness.

# Grilled Asparagus

*Most vegetables can be grilled on the indoor grill with ease and success. Asparagus is particularly outstanding because it's so easy to overcook when steaming on the stove.*

If your contact grill has more than one temperature setting, set it to high for this recipe.

**Tip**

To remove the woody ends of asparagus spears, hold each spear in the middle and break off the end with the other hand.

| | | |
|---|---|---|
| 1 | clove garlic, minced | 1 |
| 2 tbsp | freshly squeezed lemon juice | 25 mL |
| 1/2 tsp | cumin seeds | 2 mL |
| 1/4 tsp | kosher salt | 1 mL |
| 1/4 tsp | lemon pepper | 1 mL |
| 1 lb | asparagus spears, ends removed | 500 g |

1. In a small bowl, whisk together garlic, lemon juice, cumin seeds, salt and lemon pepper.
2. Place asparagus in a shallow dish and sprinkle it with marinade. Toss to coat. Marinate at room temperature for a minimum of 20 minutes or for up to 2 hours. Meanwhile, preheat contact grill.
3. Spray both sides of contact grill with vegetable cooking spray or oil. Place asparagus on grill, close lid and grill for 5 to 6 minutes, or until tender.

**Variation**
Substitute balsamic vinegar for the lemon juice and omit cumin seeds.

# Grilled Tofu

*Tofu cubes acquire a delectable crispy exterior in this grilled wonder — reminiscent of stir-fried tofu, minus the fat, of course.*

If your contact grill has more than one temperature setting, set it to high for this recipe.

## Tip

Firm or extra-firm tofu is best for the indoor grill.

Serve with rice and grilled vegetables (see page 48).

## Make Ahead

Prepare marinade up to 1 day in advance. Cover and refrigerate.

• **Preheat contact grill**

| | | |
|---|---|---|
| 2 | cloves garlic, minced | 2 |
| 1/4 cup | tamari | 50 mL |
| 1 tbsp | minced gingerroot | 15 mL |
| 1 tsp | sesame oil | 5 mL |
| 1 tsp | chili garlic sauce | 5 mL |
| 1 | package (12 oz/375 g) extra-firm tofu, cut into 1-inch (2.5 cm) cubes | 1 |

1. In a small bowl, whisk together garlic, tamari, gingerroot, sesame oil and chili garlic sauce.
2. Place tofu cubes in a shallow dish. Pour marinade over tofu and toss to coat. Cover and refrigerate for a minimum of 20 minutes or for up to 1 day. Meanwhile, preheat contact grill to high.
3. Spray both sides of contact grill with vegetable cooking spray or oil. Place tofu on grill, close lid and grill for 6 to 7 minutes, or until tofu is crisp and grill-marked.

### Variation
Use soy sauce in place of tamari.

# Grilled Vegetables

*If you love grilled vegetables (and who doesn't?), you will be wowed by how wonderful, fast and flavorful they are when prepared on your indoor grill! Let your creative juices run wild, substituting favorite vegetables, herbs or spices to suit your tastes and according to what you find in your refrigerator.*

If your contact grill has more than one temperature setting, set it to high for this recipe.

## Tips

Different vegetables require different grilling times. If you have a large enough grill, you can keep adding vegetables according to their required grilling times. If you have a smaller grill and have to grill vegetables in portions, keep them warm after grilling in a conventional oven set to 325°F (160°C).

This recipe may be halved.

| | | |
|---|---|---|
| 2 | cloves garlic, minced | 2 |
| ¼ cup | balsamic vinegar | 50 mL |
| 2½ tbsp | olive oil | 32 mL |
| 1 tsp | kosher salt | 5 mL |
| 1 tsp | dried oregano | 5 mL |
| ½ tsp | freshly ground black pepper | 2 mL |
| 2 cups | cauliflower florets (about 8 oz/250 g) | 500 mL |
| 2 cups | broccoli florets (about 8 oz/250 g) | 500 mL |
| 1 | red onion, quartered | 1 |
| 1 | green bell pepper, cut into 1-inch (2.5 cm) chunks | 1 |
| 1 | red bell pepper, cut into 1-inch (2.5 cm) chunks | 1 |
| 2 cups | mushrooms, halved | 500 mL |
| 2 | zucchini, sliced in ¼-inch (0.5 cm) rounds | 1 |
| | Fresh parsley (optional) | |

1. In a small bowl, whisk together garlic, balsamic vinegar, olive oil, salt, oregano and black pepper.

2. Place cauliflower and broccoli in a shallow dish and sprinkle with 3 tbsp (45 mL) of marinade. Toss to coat.

3. Separate onion into layers. Place in a shallow dish and sprinkle with 1 tbsp (15 mL) marinade. Toss to coat.

4. Place green and red peppers in another shallow dish and sprinkle with 1 tbsp (15 mL) marinade. Toss to coat.

Slice and marinate
vegetables up to 2 hours
in advance. Cover and
refrigerate.

5. Place mushrooms and zucchini in a fourth shallow dish and sprinkle with 1½ tbsp (22 mL) marinade. Toss to coat.

6. Marinate all vegetables at room temperature for a minimum of 20 minutes. Meanwhile, preheat contact grill.

7. Spray both sides of contact grill with vegetable cooking spray or oil. Place cauliflower and broccoli on grill, close lid and grill for 10 minutes, until tender-crisp. Transfer to a large bowl or a 13- by 9-inch (3 L) baking pan set in a 325°F (160°C) oven to keep warm.

8. Place onions on grill, brush with marinade, close lid and grill for 4 to 6 minutes. Add to bowl or baking pan to keep warm.

9. Place peppers on grill, brush with marinade, close lid and grill for 4 minutes. Add to bowl or baking pan to keep warm.

10. Place mushrooms and zucchini on grill, brush with marinade, close lid and grill for 3 minutes. Add to bowl or baking pan and toss to combine.

11. If desired, arrange decoratively on serving platter, sprinkling fresh parsley on top.

**Variation**
For a spicier version, add ½ tsp (2 mL) hot pepper flakes to the marinade.

# Low-Fat Potato Pancakes

SERVES 6

*Trade in the traditional oil-soaked variety for this appealing lower-fat version.*

If your contact grill has more than one temperature setting, set it to high for this recipe.

## Tips

Serve potato pancakes topped with sour cream (light if you prefer) or applesauce.

Yukon gold potatoes make excellent potato pancakes.

Because potato pancakes are normally fried in generous amounts of oil, it's necessary to flip them so you can spray each side of the pancakes with additional oil during the grilling process.

## Make Ahead

Grill potato pancakes up to 8 hours in advance, cool, cover and refrigerate. Reheat on a baking sheet in oven preheated to 350°F (180°C) for 20 to 30 minutes, or until heated through.

| | | |
|---|---|---|
| 8 | medium potatoes, peeled (about 2 lbs/1 kg) | 8 |
| 2 | small onions, halved | 2 |
| 2/3 cup | all-purpose flour | 150 mL |
| 2 tsp | baking powder | 10 mL |
| 1 1/2 tsp | kosher salt | 7 mL |
| 1/2 tsp | freshly ground black pepper | 2 mL |

1. In food processor fitted with grater attachment, grate potatoes (or use coarse side of box grater).

2. Place grated potatoes in a colander in the sink and rinse with cold water to remove the starch. Strain for 20 to 30 minutes. Press out any excess moisture with the back of a large spoon. Meanwhile, preheat contact grill.

3. Grate onions in food processor fitted with grater attachment (or use coarse side of box grater). Place in a large bowl.

4. After potatoes have been strained, add them to the bowl. Add the flour, baking powder, salt and pepper and mix thoroughly until well blended.

5. Spray both sides of contact grill with vegetable cooking spray or oil. Place 1/4 cup (50 mL) of batter on the grill, forming 3-inch (7.5 cm) pancakes. Spray tops of pancakes using a spray pump filled with olive oil or vegetable oil. Close lid and grill for 4 minutes. Spray tops with oil, flip and spray other side of pancakes. Grill for another 4 minutes. Repeat flipping and spraying for a total grilling time of 12 minutes.

# Sandwiches

Grilled Cheese and Asparagus Rolls . . . . . . . . . . . . . . . 52

Grilled Cheese Sandwich . . . . . . . . . . . . . . . . . . . . . . 53

Grilled French Toast . . . . . . . . . . . . . . . . . . . . . . . . 54

"Monterey" Cristo Sandwiches . . . . . . . . . . . . . . . . . . 55

Reuben Sandwiches . . . . . . . . . . . . . . . . . . . . . . . . . 56

Tuna Melts #1 . . . . . . . . . . . . . . . . . . . . . . . . . . . . 57

Tuna Melts #2 . . . . . . . . . . . . . . . . . . . . . . . . . . . . 58

Maple-Glazed Sausage Sandwiches . . . . . . . . . . . . . . . 59

Salami and Red Pepper Panini with Asiago . . . . . . . . . 60

Smoked Cheese and Turkey Breast Panini . . . . . . . . . . 61

Three-Meat Panini with Provolone . . . . . . . . . . . . . . . 62

Grilled Mango and Brie Quesadillas . . . . . . . . . . . . . . 63

Mexican Cheese Quesadillas . . . . . . . . . . . . . . . . . . . 64

Chicken and Monterey Jack Quesadillas . . . . . . . . . . . 65

Pita Pizzas . . . . . . . . . . . . . . . . . . . . . . . . . . . . . . . 66

# Grilled Cheese and Asparagus Rolls

*The sharp cold-pack Cheddar is great melted on this different take of the classic grilled cheese and asparagus roll.*

If your contact grill has more than one temperature setting, set it to high for this recipe.

**Tip**

Sharp cold-pack Cheddar can be found alongside other packaged cheeses in the dairy section of the supermarket.

**Make Ahead**

Trim and steam asparagus up to 1 hour in advance. Cover and refrigerate.

• **Preheat contact grill**

| | | |
|---|---|---|
| 4 | Kaiser rolls | 4 |
| 1 cup | grated sharp cold-pack Cheddar cheese | 250 mL |
| 8 | spears asparagus, trimmed and steamed | 8 |
| 1/4 | red bell pepper, thinly sliced | 1/4 |
| | Freshly ground black pepper (optional) | |
| 2 tsp | butter, at room temperature, divided | 10 mL |

1. Slice Kaiser rolls in half and place cut-side down on grill. With lid open, grill for 1 minute.
2. Evenly divide the cheese, asparagus and red pepper among the rolls to make four sandwiches. Sprinkle with pepper, if using.
3. Spread 1/2 teaspoon (2 mL) of butter on the outside of each roll, making sure to butter both sides.
4. Place sandwiches on contact grill and close tightly. Grill for 2 to 3 minutes, or until golden brown and crisp.

**Variations**

Sprinkle 1 tbsp (15 mL) chopped fresh basil on top of the cheese.

In place of fresh steamed asparagus, used drained pickled asparagus.

# Grilled Cheese Sandwich

**SERVES 4**

*This perennial comfort food, given two thumbs up by my 12-year-old son, Evan, is sublime when prepared on the indoor grill. Not only does it require less butter than the traditional pan-fried grilled cheese, but the indoor grill produces the ultimate crispy outer surface.*

If your contact grill has more than one temperature setting, set it to high for this recipe.

## Tips

Serve with creamy tomato soup for a homey lunch.

If using unsliced bread, slice about ½ inch (1 cm) thick for best results.

## Make Ahead

Buy pre-shredded cheese from the supermarket to speed things up, or shred cheese yourself up to 8 hours in advance. Place in a resealable plastic bag and refrigerate.

- Preheat contact grill

| | | |
|---|---|---|
| 1 | clove garlic, minced (optional) | 1 |
| 1 tbsp | Dijon mayonnaise (optional) | 15 mL |
| 8 | slices whole wheat bread | 8 |
| 8 oz | Cheddar cheese, shredded (about 2 cups/500 mL) | 250 g |
| 1 | large tomato, thinly sliced | 1 |
| 8 tsp | butter, at room temperature, divided | 30 mL |

1. In small bowl, stir together garlic and mayonnaise, if using.
2. On each of 4 slices of bread, spread mayonnaise mixture, if using, dividing it evenly. Top with one-quarter of the cheese, then with one-quarter of the tomato slices. Top the sandwiches with the remaining 4 slices of bread.
3. Spread 2 tsp (10 mL) butter on the outside of each sandwich, making sure to butter both sides.
4. Place sandwiches on contact grill and close tightly. Grill for 2 to 3 minutes, or until golden brown and crisp.

### Variation
Use thinly sliced dill pickle in place of tomato.

# Grilled French Toast

*While not technically a sandwich, French toast makes an excellent entrée for Sunday brunch and is fabulously easy to prepare on the indoor grill. My husband, Ari Marantz, always makes the French toast in our house and created this scrumptious recipe for the indoor grill.*

If your contact grill has more than one temperature setting, set it to high for this recipe.

## Tip

These taste so much like traditional fried French toast that you can barely tell the difference, or that you've used much less butter for grilling.

• **Preheat contact grill**

| | | |
|---|---|---|
| 4 | eggs | 4 |
| 1 cup | milk | 250 mL |
| 1 tbsp | Irish cream liqueur | 15 mL |
| 8 | slices egg bread (1/2-inch/1 cm thick) | 8 |
| | Salt and freshly ground black pepper to taste | |
| 1 tsp | butter, melted, divided | 5 mL |
| | Pure maple syrup | |

1. In a medium bowl, beat eggs. Stir in milk and liqueur and blend well.

2. Pour half of the egg mixture into a large shallow dish. Place 4 slices of bread in the dish to soak in the egg mixture until it is absorbed (about 5 to 10 minutes), flipping the bread halfway through. Season with salt and pepper.

3. Brush contact grill with 1/2 tsp (2 mL) of the melted butter. Lay the 4 soaked slices of bread on grill. Close lid and grill for 5 to 6 minutes, or until golden brown and crisp. Meanwhile, place the other 4 slices of bread in the egg mixture to soak as above. When the grilled slices are done, transfer them to a plate or baking pan set in a 325°F (160°C) oven to keep warm while the other slices are grilling.

4. Brush contact grill with the remaining 1/2 tsp (2 mL) melted butter. Lay the second set of soaked slices of bread on grill, close lid and grill as above.

5. Serve hot with maple syrup.

### Variation

French toast also tastes great made with Amaretto, which gives it an alluring almond flavor. Omit the liqueur if desired.

# "Monterey" Cristo Sandwiches

**SERVES 4**

*Traditional Monte Cristo sandwiches are given a Mexican twist when prepared in tortillas on the grill. These sandwiches are ideal for a relaxing weekend brunch.*

If your contact grill has more than one temperature setting, set it to high for this recipe.

## Tip

These tortilla sandwiches require a longer grilling time to ensure that the egg mixture is cooked through.

## Make Ahead

Shred cheese and slice vegetables and garlic sausage up to 8 hours in advance. Place in a resealable plastic bag and refrigerate.

• Preheat contact grill

| | | |
|---|---|---|
| 1 | egg | 1 |
| ¹⁄₄ cup | milk | 50 mL |
| 4 | 8-inch (20 cm) tortillas | 4 |
| 4 oz | smoked, fully cooked garlic sausage, thinly sliced | 125 g |
| 2 | drained pickled jalapeño peppers, minced (about 2 tbsp/25 mL) | 2 |
| ¹⁄₂ | green bell pepper, thinly sliced | ¹⁄₂ |
| 4 oz | Monterey Jack cheese, shredded (about 1 cup/250 mL) | 125 g |
| | Salsa | |

1. In a large shallow dish, beat eggs. Stir in milk and blend well.
2. Cover half of each tortilla with one-quarter each of the sausage, jalapeño, bell peppers and cheese. Fold tortillas over to make half moons.
3. Soak each tortilla for 5 minutes in egg mixture, then use a pastry brush to paint the top of the tortillas with egg mixture.
4. Spray both sides of contact grill with vegetable cooking spray or oil. Place tortillas on grill, folded side closest to the front edge. Close lid. Grill for 5 to 6 minutes, or until golden brown and crisp.
5. Slice each tortilla into three triangles and serve with salsa.

### Variations

Use jalapeño Monterey Jack cheese in place of plain.

Use sliced ham in place of garlic sausage.

# Reuben Sandwiches

One of the most popular deli sandwiches, the Reuben is a cinch to create at home on the indoor grill.

If your contact grill has more than one temperature setting, set it to high for this recipe.

**Tip**

This recipe easily doubles or can be made for one. Per sandwich, use 3 oz (90 g) corned beef, $\frac{1}{2}$ oz (15 g) Swiss cheese, 2 tbsp (25 mL) drained sauerkraut and $1\frac{1}{2}$ tsp (7 mL) Thousand Island dressing.

• Preheat contact grill

| 12 oz | shaved corned beef | 375 g |
|---|---|---|
| 8 | slices rye bread | 8 |
| 4 | slices Swiss cheese (about 2 oz/60 g) | 4 |
| $\frac{1}{2}$ cup | drained sauerkraut | 125 mL |
| 2 tbsp | Thousand Island dressing | 25 mL |
| 4 tsp | vegetable or olive oil | 20 mL |

1. Divide the corned beef among 4 slices of bread. Top each with 1 slice of Swiss cheese and 2 tbsp (25 mL) of sauerkraut. Spread Thousand Island dressing on each of the 4 top slices of bread.

2. Close the sandwiches and brush the oil on the outsides of them.

3. Place sandwiches on contact grill and close tightly. Grill for 2 to 3 minutes, or until cheese is melted and sandwich is golden brown.

**Variation**
Brush the outsides of the sandwiches with melted butter instead of oil.

# Tuna Melts #1

*A family favorite lunch is made even better when grilled. English muffins make this sandwich king.*

If your contact grill has more than one temperature setting, set it to high for this recipe.

**Make Ahead**

Prepare tuna mixture and shred cheese up to 8 hours in advance. Cover and refrigerate.

- **Preheat contact grill**

| | | |
|---|---|---|
| 2 | cans (each 6 oz/170 g) tuna, drained | 2 |
| 3 tbsp | mayonnaise | 45 mL |
| 1 tbsp | chopped fresh parsley | 15 mL |
| 1 tsp | prepared horseradish | 5 mL |
| 1/4 tsp | paprika | 1 mL |
| 1/4 tsp | salt | 1 mL |
| 1/4 tsp | freshly ground black pepper | 1 mL |
| 6 | English muffins | 6 |
| 1/2 cup | shredded Cheddar cheese (about 2 oz/60 g) | 125 mL |

1. In a medium bowl, stir together tuna, mayonnaise, parsley, horseradish, paprika, salt and pepper.

2. Split open English muffins. Spread the tuna mixture on half of each English muffin, dividing it evenly. Top each with cheddar cheese. Close the sandwiches.

3. Spray both sides of contact grill with vegetable cooking spray or oil. Place sandwiches on grill and close lid tightly. Grill for 2 to 3 minutes, or until golden brown and crisp.

**Variations**

Use canned drained salmon in place of tuna, and shredded Swiss cheese in place of Cheddar.

Add thinly sliced dill pickle or tomato to the sandwich before grilling.

# Tuna Melts #2

*Tuna melts make an easy lunch or, paired with soup, a midweek supper.*

If your contact grill has more than one temperature setting, set it to high for this recipe.

## Tip

For a more wholesome lunch, use whole wheat English muffins, light Thousand Island dressing and lower-fat Cheddar or light mozzarella cheese.

## Make Ahead

Prepare tuna mixture and shred cheese up to 8 hours in advance. Cover and refrigerate.

• **Preheat contact grill**

| | | |
|---|---|---|
| 2 | cans (each 6 oz/170 g) tuna, drained | 2 |
| 3 tbsp | Thousand Island dressing | 45 mL |
| 1/2 tsp | chili powder | 2 mL |
| 1/4 tsp | freshly ground black pepper | 1 mL |
| 1 | green onion, minced | 1 |
| 6 | English muffins | 6 |
| 2 | dill or sweet pickles, thinly sliced into rounds 1/8 inch (2.5 mm) thick | 2 |
| 1/2 cup | shredded Cheddar cheese (about 2 oz/60 g) | 125 mL |

1. In a medium bowl, stir together tuna, Thousand Island dressing, chili powder, pepper and green onion.
2. Split open English muffins. Spread the tuna mixture on half of each English muffin, dividing it evenly. Top each with pickle slices and cheese. Close the sandwiches.
3. Spray both sides of contact grill with vegetable cooking spray or oil. Place sandwiches on grill and close lid tightly. Grill for 2 to 3 minutes, or until golden brown and crisp.

## Variation

Use peppercorn ranch dressing in place of Thousand Island dressing and omit freshly ground pepper.

# Maple-Glazed Sausage Sandwiches

*You will be amazed at how much fat drips off when you grill sausage on your indoor grill. You'll never want to return to pan frying!*

If your contact grill has more than one temperature setting, set it to high for this recipe.

**Tip**

Pure maple syrup is necessary for this recipe.

- Preheat contact grill

| | | |
|---|---|---|
| 3 tbsp | pure maple syrup | 45 mL |
| 1 tbsp | cider vinegar | 15 mL |
| 1 tbsp | Dijon mustard | 15 mL |
| 6 | Bratwurst sausages (about 1 lb/500 g) | 6 |
| 6 | oblong Italian buns | 6 |

1. In a small bowl, stir together maple syrup, vinegar and mustard.
2. Cut sausages in half lengthwise. Place cut-side down on contact grill and brush with half of the maple syrup glaze. Close lid and grill for 8 minutes. Flip sausages, brush on remaining glaze, close lid and grill for another 4 minutes, or until no longer pink inside.
3. Slice buns in half lengthwise, almost but not all the way through, and fill with sausage. Serve warm.

**Variations**

Use other favorite buns, such as whole wheat or sesame seed hot dog buns, in place of crusty Italian buns.

If desired, lightly toast buns, cut-side down, on the grill for about 1 minute.

# Salami and Red Pepper Panini with Asiago

SERVES 4

*Panini is a sensational Italian sandwich filled with meat and cheese and grilled to perfection. The indoor grill is just right for the job! Adjust the amount of meat according to your tastes.*

If your contact grill has more than one temperature setting, set it to high for this recipe.

## Tip
If you can't find panini buns, look for Portuguese buns or other crusty white buns.

## Make Ahead
Prepare dressing up to 1 day in advance. Cover and refrigerate. Sandwiches can be assembled, wrapped tightly with plastic wrap and refrigerated for up to 2 hours before grilling.

• Preheat contact grill

| | | |
|---|---|---|
| $\frac{1}{4}$ | red bell pepper | $\frac{1}{4}$ |
| $\frac{1}{4}$ | red onion | $\frac{1}{4}$ |
| 4 | Italian panini buns | 4 |
| 4 to 6 oz | Calabrese salami, sliced | 120 to 180 g |
| 4 to 6 oz | glazed pepper salami, sliced | 120 to 180 g |
| 4 to 6 oz | Hungarian salami, sliced | 120 to 180 g |
| 4 | slices Asiago cheese (about 2 oz/60 g) | 4 |

### Dressing
| | | |
|---|---|---|
| 1 tbsp | olive oil | 15 mL |
| 1 tsp | red wine vinegar | 5 mL |
| 1 | clove garlic, minced | 1 |
| 1 tbsp | chopped fresh oregano (or 1 tsp/5 mL dried) | 15 mL |

1. *Prepare dressing:* In a small bowl, whisk together olive oil, vinegar, garlic and oregano.
2. Grill pepper and onion on contact grill for 3 to 4 minutes, or until tender. Cool and chop.
3. Cut buns in half. Spread one-quarter of the dressing on the bottom half of each bun. Add the three salamis and the cheese slices to each and sprinkle with red pepper and red onion. Close buns.
4. Place sandwiches on grill and close tightly. Grill for 2 to 3 minutes, or until cheese is melted and sandwich is golden brown.

### Variation
Use other salamis or hams, if desired, in place of the suggested meats.

# Smoked Cheese and Turkey Breast Panini

SERVES 4

*Try to find naturally wood-smoked cheese for this sandwich. Wood-smoking imbues the cheese with a deep smoky essence.*

If your contact grill has more than one temperature setting, set it to high for this recipe.

## Tip

Soak sun-dried tomatoes in boiling water for 20 minutes. Remove from water, pat dry and chop or cut with scissors.

## Make Ahead

Prepare sun-dried tomatoes up to 8 hours in advance. Place in a resealable plastic bag and refrigerate. Sandwiches can be assembled, wrapped tightly with plastic wrap and refrigerated for up to 2 hours before grilling.

• Preheat contact grill

| | | |
|---|---|---|
| 4 | Italian panini buns | 4 |
| 4 tsp | grainy mustard | 20 mL |
| 16 oz | roasted turkey breast, shaved | 500 g |
| 8 | slices smoked Cheddar cheese (about 4 oz/125 g) | 8 |
| 4 | sun-dried tomatoes, soaked and chopped (see tip, at left) | 4 |
| 4 | large basil leaves, chopped | 4 |

1. Cut buns in half. Spread 1 tsp (5 mL) grainy mustard on the bottom half of each bun. Top with 4 oz (125 g) turkey breast, 2 slices Cheddar, one quarter of the chopped sun-dried tomatoes (about 1 tsp/5 mL) and one-quarter of the chopped basil leaves. Close buns.

2. Spray both sides of contact grill with vegetable cooking spray or oil. Place sandwiches on grill and close lid tightly. Grill for 2 to 3 minutes, or until cheese is melted and sandwich is golden brown.

### Variation
Use smoked turkey breast and plain cheddar cheese if you must!

# Three-Meat Panini with Provolone

*A simple sandwich is taken to great new heights when prepared on the indoor grill! Serve with minestrone for an Italian-themed lunch.*

If your contact grill has more than one temperature setting, set it to high for this recipe.

## Tip
Cervalat salami is a French soft salami encrusted with black peppercorns.

## Make Ahead
Prepare dressing up to 1 day in advance. Cover and refrigerate.

• Preheat contact grill

| | | |
|---|---|---|
| 1 | clove garlic, minced | 1 |
| 3 tbsp | chopped black olives | 45 mL |
| 2 tbsp | olive oil | 25 mL |
| 2 tbsp | chopped fresh oregano (or 2 tsp/10 mL dried) | 25 mL |
| 1 tsp | balsamic vinegar | 5 mL |
| 4 | Italian panini buns | 4 |
| 4 oz | Calabrese salami, sliced | 125 g |
| 4 oz | cervelat salami, sliced | 125 g |
| 4 oz | prosciutto, thinly sliced | 125 g |
| 4 | slices provolone cheese (about 2 oz/60 g) | 4 |

1. In a small bowl, whisk together garlic, olives, olive oil, oregano and vinegar.

2. Cut buns in half. Spread one-quarter of the oil and vinegar dressing on the bottom half of each bun. Top with the salamis, prosciutto and provolone. Close buns.

3. Spray both sides of contact grill with vegetable cooking spray or oil. Place sandwiches on grill and close lid tightly. Grill for 2 to 3 minutes, or until cheese is melted and sandwich is golden brown.

## Variation
Use Hungarian salami, glazed pepper salami, or different hams in place of the suggested meats.

# Grilled Mango and Brie Quesadillas

*This marriage of magnificent mango and creamy Brie cheese is a mouthwatering light lunch, or it can do double duty as an attention-grabbing appetizer.*

If your contact grill has more than one temperature setting, set it to high for this recipe.

## Tips

Make sure your mango is ripe. To speed up the process, place in a paper bag with bananas, but check frequently to prevent over-ripening!

When grilling quesadillas, always position the folded side closest to the front edge to prevent cheese from running down into the drip tray.

## Make Ahead

Prepare mango salsa up to 2 hours in advance. Cover with plastic wrap and refrigerate.

• Preheat contact grill

| | | |
|---|---|---|
| 1 | mango, peeled and chopped | 1 |
| 1 | jalapeño pepper, seeded and minced | 1 |
| ¼ cup | minced red onion | 50 mL |
| ¼ cup | chopped fresh cilantro | 50 mL |
| | Juice of 1 lime | |
| 8 oz | Brie cheese, thinly sliced | 250 g |
| 8 | 10-inch (25 cm) tortillas | 8 |

1. In a small bowl, combine mango, jalapeño, onion and cilantro. Add lime juice, mixing well to combine.
2. Divide Brie evenly among the tortillas, laying it on the lower half. Divide the mango salsa evenly on top of Brie. Fold each tortilla in half.
3. Spray both sides of contact grill with vegetable cooking spray or oil. Place quesadillas on grill with folded side closest to the front edge. Close lid. Grill for 2 to 3 minutes, or until golden brown and crisp.
4. Slice each quesadilla into two triangles.

### Variation
Replace jalapeño pepper with 1 tsp (5 mL) chili powder.

# Mexican Cheese Quesadillas

*Quesadillas lend themselves to creativity and taste. Express yourself with this simple lunch or appetizer fare by highlighting your favorite cheeses, herbs or condiments.*

If your contact grill has more than one temperature setting, set it to high for this recipe.

## Tips

Sharp cold-pack Cheddar is splendid for melting. It must be very cold to grate easily.

Each quesadilla may be sliced into 8 triangles to serve as appetizers.

## Make Ahead

Quesadillas can be assembled, placed on a tray, covered tightly with plastic wrap and refrigerated for up to 2 hours before grilling.

• Preheat contact grill

| | | |
|---|---|---|
| 1/2 cup | grated sharp cold-pack Cheddar cheese (about 2 oz/60g) | 125 mL |
| 1/2 cup | shredded Monterey Jack cheese (about 2 oz/60 g) | 125 mL |
| 4 | 10-inch (25 cm) tortillas | 4 |
| 2 | drained pickled jalapeño peppers, minced (about 2 tbsp/25 mL) | 2 |
| 2 tbsp | chopped fresh cilantro | 25 mL |
| 2 tbsp | minced green onion (optional) | 25 mL |
| 1/2 tsp | ground coriander | 2 mL |

1. In a small bowl, combine Cheddar and Jack cheeses. Divide evenly on top of 2 tortillas.

2. Sprinkle pickled jalapeño, cilantro, green onion, if using, and coriander over cheese, distributing evenly. Top with the remaining 2 tortillas.

3. Spray both sides of contact grill with vegetable cooking spray or oil. Place quesadillas on grill with folded side closest to the front edge. Close lid. Grill for 2 to 3 minutes, or until golden brown and crisp.

4. Slice each quesadilla into quarters, serving two portions to each person.

## Variations

Use jalapeño Monterey Jack cheese in place of plain, and omit pickled jalapeños.

Use old Cheddar in place of cold-pack Cheddar.

Mexican Steak (page 103)
*Overleaf:* Asian Steak Noodle Salad (page 36)

# Chicken and Monterey Jack Quesadillas

**MAKES
8 QUESADILLAS**

*Quesadillas are perfect for casual entertaining, as a quick suppertime solution or as uncomplicated appetizers before a dinner party.*

If your contact grill has more than one temperature setting, set it to high for this recipe.

### Tips

Serve with salsa, sour cream and guacamole.

Use jalapeño Monterey Jack cheese in place of plain Monterey Jack cheese.

### Make Ahead

Grill chicken up to 1 day in advance. Cover and refrigerate. Assemble quesadillas just before serving.

Barbecued Chicken with a Difference (page 108)

| | | |
|---|---|---|
| 1 tbsp | chili powder | 15 mL |
| 1½ tsp | dried onion flakes | 7 mL |
| ½ tsp | ground cumin | 2 mL |
| ½ tsp | garlic powder | 2 mL |
| ½ tsp | dried oregano | 2 mL |
| ½ tsp | salt | 2 mL |
| ¼ tsp | cayenne pepper | 1 mL |
| 1 lb | boneless, skinless chicken breasts, sliced into 1-inch (2.5 cm) pieces | 500 g |
| 8 | 10-inch (25 cm) tortillas | 8 |
| 8 oz | Monterey Jack cheese, shredded (about 2 cups/500 mL) | 250 g |
| ¼ cup | chopped fresh cilantro | 50 mL |
| 2 | green onions, minced | 2 |

1. In a small bowl, stir together chili powder, onion flakes, cumin, garlic powder, oregano, salt and cayenne.

2. In a large bowl, spread this rub on chicken pieces, ensuring all pieces are completely covered. Cover and refrigerate for 20 minutes or for up to 1 day. Meanwhile, preheat contact grill.

3. Spray both sides of contact grill with vegetable cooking spray or oil. Place chicken on grill, close lid and grill for 5 to 6 minutes, or until chicken is no longer pink inside and reaches an internal temperature of 170°F (75°C). Wipe grill clean.

4. *Assemble quesadillas:* Onto half of each tortilla, place about one-eighth each of chicken and cheese. Sprinkle with cilantro and green onions. Fold tortillas over to make half moons.

5. Spray both sides of contact grill with vegetable cooking spray or oil. Place quesadillas on grill with folded side closest to the front edge. Close lid. Grill for 2 to 3 minutes, or until golden brown and crisp.

# Pita Pizzas

**SERVES 4**

*This pita version is filled, then grilled, and produces a delightful and delicious crispy "crust."*

If your contact grill has more than one temperature setting, set it to high for this recipe.

## Tip
Whole wheat pitas hold together better than plain white pitas when grilled.

## Make Ahead
Shred cheese and slice vegetables and pepperoni up to 8 hours in advance. Place in a resealable plastic bag and refrigerate.

• Preheat contact grill

| | | |
|---|---|---|
| 4 oz | pepperoni, thinly sliced | 125 g |
| 1/2 | red bell pepper, thinly sliced | 1/2 |
| 1/2 | green bell pepper, thinly sliced | 1/2 |
| 1/2 cup | sliced mushrooms | 125 mL |
| 4 | large whole wheat pitas | 4 |
| 1/2 cup | salsa or thick pasta sauce | 125 mL |
| 3/4 cup | shredded mozzarella cheese | 175 mL |
| 1 tsp | dried oregano | 5 mL |

1. Spray both sides of contact grill with vegetable cooking spray or oil. Place pepperoni slices, red and green peppers and mushrooms on grill. Close tightly and grill for 3 minutes, or until lightly browned. Remove from grill and set aside.

2. Cut pitas in half crosswise and gently open to form pocket. Spread about 1 tbsp (15 mL) salsa inside each pita half. Divide the pepperoni, red and green pepper slices, mushrooms and cheese evenly and place inside the pita halves. Season with oregano.

3. Spray both sides of contact grill with vegetable cooking spray or oil. Place pita halves on grill with folded side closest to the front edge. Close lid. Grill for 2 to 3 minutes, or until golden brown and crisp.

### Variation
Replace the suggested ingredients with your favorite pizza toppings.

# Burgers

Ultimate Hamburger. . . . . . . . . . . . . . . . . . . . . . . . . . . 68

All-in-One Cheeseburgers. . . . . . . . . . . . . . . . . . . . . . 69

Seasoned Beef Burgers . . . . . . . . . . . . . . . . . . . . . . . 70

Caesar Burgers. . . . . . . . . . . . . . . . . . . . . . . . . . . . . 71

French Quarter Burgers. . . . . . . . . . . . . . . . . . . . . . . 72

Smoky Mexican Burgers . . . . . . . . . . . . . . . . . . . . . . 73

Curry Beef Burgers . . . . . . . . . . . . . . . . . . . . . . . . . . 74

Thai Curry Burgers . . . . . . . . . . . . . . . . . . . . . . . . . . 75

Burgers with Horseradish
    and Caramelized Onions. . . . . . . . . . . . . . . . . . . 76

Italian Veal Burgers. . . . . . . . . . . . . . . . . . . . . . . . . 78

Sausage Burgers. . . . . . . . . . . . . . . . . . . . . . . . . . . . 79

Portobello Mushroom Burgers . . . . . . . . . . . . . . . . . 80

Hickory Chicken Burgers . . . . . . . . . . . . . . . . . . . . . 82

Tarragon Mustard Chicken Burgers . . . . . . . . . . . . . 83

Cheesy Turkey Burgers . . . . . . . . . . . . . . . . . . . . . . 84

Creamy Turkey Burgers . . . . . . . . . . . . . . . . . . . . . . 85

Pimiento Turkey Burgers . . . . . . . . . . . . . . . . . . . . . 86

Turkey Mango Burgers . . . . . . . . . . . . . . . . . . . . . . 87

Turkey Thyme Burgers . . . . . . . . . . . . . . . . . . . . . . 88

# Ultimate Hamburger

*The indoor grill makes barbecuing burgers a year-round pleasure and allows you to lose the fat, but not the flavor.*

If your contact grill has more than one temperature setting, set it to high for this recipe.

## Tips

Garnish with your favorite toppings, such as Dijon mustard, lettuce, pickles and tomatoes.

The dried onion soup mix is salty enough that additional salt is not necessary.

## Make Ahead

Prepare burgers up to 8 hours in advance. Wrap tightly in plastic wrap and refrigerate until ready to grill.

• Preheat contact grill

| | | |
|---|---|---|
| 1 lb | lean ground beef | 500 g |
| 1 | egg, beaten | 1 |
| 1 | clove garlic, minced | 1 |
| ½ cup | dry bread crumbs | 125 mL |
| ⅓ cup | barbecue sauce | 75 mL |
| 3 tbsp | dry onion soup mix (about ½ envelope) | 45 mL |
| 6 | Kaiser buns | 6 |

1. In a large bowl, combine beef, egg, garlic, bread crumbs, barbecue sauce and onion soup mix. Mix well. Shape into 6 patties ½ inch (1 cm) thick.
2. Spray both sides of contact grill with vegetable cooking spray or oil. Place patties on grill, close lid and grill for 5 to 7minutes, or until no longer pink and internal temperature has reached 160°F (71°C).
3. Serve in Kaiser buns.

### Variation
Use an equal amount of ground chicken in place of ground beef and grill for 6 to 8 minutes, to an internal temperature of 175°F (80°C).

# All-in-One Cheeseburgers

**MAKES
6 BURGERS**

*Since indoor grilling does not lend itself to preparing the usual cheeseburger (with cheese melted on top), I devised this recipe that incorporates cheese right into the ground beef. Say cheese!*

If your contact grill has more than one temperature setting, set it to high for this recipe.

## Tips

Garnish with toppings such as salsa, lettuce, olives and tomatoes.

The processed cheese spread imparts a creamy cheese essence to the burgers.

## Make Ahead

Prepare burgers up to 8 hours in advance. Wrap tightly in plastic wrap and refrigerate until ready to grill.

• **Preheat contact grill**

| | | |
|---|---|---|
| 1 lb | lean ground beef | 500 g |
| 2 | cloves garlic, minced | 2 |
| 1 | egg, beaten | 1 |
| 1/3 cup | processed cheese spread | 75 mL |
| 1/4 cup | quick-cooking rolled oats | 50 mL |
| 1 tbsp | dried onion flakes | 15 mL |
| 1 tbsp | Worcestershire sauce | 15 mL |
| 1/2 tsp | dry mustard powder | 2 mL |
| 1/4 tsp | kosher salt | 1 mL |
| 1/4 tsp | freshly ground black pepper | 1 mL |
| 6 | whole wheat buns | 6 |

**1.** In a large bowl, combine beef, garlic, egg, cheese spread, oats, onion flakes, Worcestershire sauce, mustard powder, salt and pepper. Mix well. With wet hands, shape into 6 patties 1/2 inch (1 cm) thick.

**2.** Spray both sides of contact grill with vegetable cooking spray or oil. Place patties on grill, close lid and grill for 5 to 7 minutes, or until no longer pink and internal temperature has reached 160°F (71°C).

**3.** Serve in whole wheat buns.

### Variation
Use an equal amount of ground chicken in place of ground beef and grill 6 to 8 minutes, to an internal temperature of 175°F (80°C).

# Seasoned Beef Burgers

**MAKES
6 BURGERS**

*The secret ingredient —
sour-cream-and-onion
potato chip crumbs —
pack in the flavor and
make these burgers a
kid favorite.*

If your contact grill
has more than one
temperature setting,
set it to high for
this recipe.

## Tip

If you ever run out of dry
bread crumbs, you can
always use potato chips
in a crunch. They're
packed with salt, so adjust
recipe accordingly. Try
different varieties, such
as barbecue, ketchup or
all-dressed.

## Make Ahead

Prepare burgers up
to 8 hours in advance.
Wrap tightly in plastic
wrap and refrigerate
until ready to grill.

• **Preheat contact grill**

| 1 lb | lean ground beef | 500 g |
|---|---|---|
| 2 | cloves garlic, minced | 2 |
| 1 | egg, beaten | 1 |
| 1/3 cup | sour-cream-and-onion potato chip crumbs | 75 mL |
| 2 tbsp | peppercorn ranch dressing | 25 mL |
| 1/2 tsp | dried parsley flakes | 2 mL |
| 1/4 tsp | freshly ground black pepper | 1 mL |
| 6 | whole wheat Kaiser buns | 6 |

1. In a large bowl, combine beef, garlic, egg, potato chip crumbs, dressing, parsley and pepper. Mix well. Shape into 6 patties 1/2 inch (1 cm) thick.
2. Spray both sides of contact grill with vegetable cooking spray or oil. Place patties on grill, close lid and grill for 5 to 7 minutes, or until no longer pink and internal temperature has reached 160°F (71°C).
3. Serve in whole wheat Kaiser buns and garnish with your favorite toppings.

### Variation
Use half ground veal and half ground beef in place of all ground beef.

# Caesar Burgers

**MAKES
6 BURGERS**

*What do you get when you cross Caesar salad with hamburgers? A fresh twist to wow family and friends.*

If your contact grill has more than one temperature setting, set it to high for this recipe.

## Tips

Garnish with red onion, bacon strips and sautéed mushrooms.

If really pinched for time, use about 2 tbsp (25 mL) bottled Caesar dressing in place of homemade.

## Make Ahead

Prepare burgers up to 8 hours in advance. Wrap tightly in plastic wrap and refrigerate until ready to grill.

- Preheat contact grill

| | | |
|---|---|---|
| 1 lb | lean ground beef | 500 g |
| 1 | egg, beaten | 1 |
| 1 | shallot, finely minced (about 1/4 cup/50 mL) | 1 |
| 1/2 cup | Caesar salad–flavored croutons, finely crushed | 125 mL |
| 1/4 cup | freshly grated Parmesan cheese | 50 mL |
| 6 | crusty Italian buns | 6 |

**Dressing**

| | | |
|---|---|---|
| 2 | cloves garlic, minced | 2 |
| 1 1/2 tsp | Worcestershire sauce | 7 mL |
| 1 1/2 tsp | olive oil | 7 mL |
| 1 tsp | freshly squeezed lemon juice | 5 mL |
| 1 tsp | red wine vinegar | 5 mL |
| 3/4 tsp | dry mustard powder | 4 mL |
| 1/2 tsp | kosher salt | 2 mL |
| 1/4 tsp | freshly ground black pepper | 1 mL |

1. *Prepare dressing:* In a small bowl, whisk together garlic, Worcestershire sauce, olive oil, lemon juice, vinegar, mustard powder, salt and pepper.
2. In a large bowl, combine beef, egg, shallot, crouton crumbs, dressing and Parmesan cheese. Shape into 6 patties 1/2 inch (1 cm) thick.
3. Spray both sides of contact grill with vegetable cooking spray or oil. Place patties on grill, close lid and grill for 5 to 7 minutes, or until no longer pink and internal temperature has reached 160°F (71°C).
4. Serve in crusty Italian buns.

**Variation**
Use an equal amount of ground pork in place of ground beef.

# French Quarter Burgers

*French flavors take this grilled hamburger up a notch.*

If your contact grill has more than one temperature setting, set it to high for this recipe.

## Tips

Garnish with your favorite toppings, such as Dijon mustard, sliced red onion and pickles.

*Herbes de Provence* is an assortment of dried herbs used extensively in southern France and usually includes a combination of marjoram, basil, rosemary, thyme and fennel. Look for it in the herb and spice section of well-stocked supermarkets, specialty foods or bulk stores.

## Make Ahead

Prepare burgers up to 8 hours in advance. Wrap tightly in plastic wrap and refrigerate until ready to grill.

• **Preheat contact grill**

| | | |
|---|---|---|
| 1 lb | lean ground beef | 500 g |
| 1 | egg, beaten | 1 |
| 1 | green onion, finely minced | 1 |
| 1 | clove garlic, minced | 1 |
| ¼ cup | dry bread crumbs | 50 mL |
| 1 tbsp | Dijon mustard | 15 mL |
| 1 tbsp | Worcestershire sauce | 15 mL |
| 1 tsp | dried *herbes de Provence* (see tip, at left) | 5 mL |
| ½ tsp | kosher salt | 2 mL |
| ¼ tsp | freshly ground black pepper | 1 mL |
| 6 | crusty white buns | 6 |

1. In a large bowl, combine beef, egg, onion, garlic, bread crumbs, Dijon mustard, Worcestershire sauce, *herbes de Provence*, salt and pepper. Mix well. Shape into 6 patties ½ inch (1 cm) thick.
2. Spray both sides of contact grill with vegetable cooking spray or oil. Place patties on grill, close lid and grill for 5 to 7 minutes, or until no longer pink and internal temperature has reached 160°F (71°C).
3. Serve in crusty white buns.

### Variation
Use an equal amount of ground turkey in place of ground beef and grill for 6 to 8 minutes, to an internal temperature of 175°F (80°C).

# Smoky Mexican Burgers

*You'll love the seductive smokiness of these burgers.*

If your contact grill has more than one temperature setting, set it to high for this recipe.

## Tips

Garnish with your favorite taco toppings, such as salsa, shredded lettuce, grated cheddar cheese and chopped tomatoes.

Spicy chipotles are the latest rage. The dried and smoked jalapeño peppers are often canned in tomato adobo sauce. Many new products such as flavored hot pepper and barbecue sauces conveniently impart the seductive smoky essence of chipotles.

## Make Ahead

Prepare burgers up to 8 hours in advance. Wrap tightly in plastic wrap and refrigerate until ready to grill.

• **Preheat contact grill**

| | | |
|---|---|---|
| 1 lb | lean ground beef | 500 g |
| 1 | egg | 1 |
| 1 | clove garlic, minced | 1 |
| 1/4 cup | tortilla chip crumbs | 50 mL |
| 3 tbsp | ketchup | 45 mL |
| 2 tbsp | finely minced onion | 25 mL |
| 2 tbsp | chopped fresh cilantro | 25 mL |
| 1 1/2 tsp | hot pepper sauce with chipotle | 7 mL |
| 1/2 tsp | cumin seeds | 2 mL |
| 1/2 tsp | kosher salt | 2 mL |
| 1/4 tsp | freshly ground black pepper | 1 mL |
| 6 | hamburger buns or hard taco shells | 6 |

1. In a large bowl, combine beef, egg, garlic, tortilla chip crumbs, ketchup, onion, cilantro, hot pepper sauce, cumin, salt and pepper. Mix well. Shape into 6 patties 1/2 inch (1 cm) thick.

2. Spray both sides of contact grill with vegetable cooking spray or oil. Place patties on grill, close lid and grill for 5 to 7 minutes, or until no longer pink and internal temperature has reached 160°F (71°C).

3. Serve in hamburger buns or slice burgers in half and serve in taco shells.

### Variation
Use an equal amount of minced chipotle chilies in adobo sauce in place of the hot pepper sauce with chipotle.

# Curry Beef Burgers

*These curry-spiked burgers will please curry enthusiasts, and tempt curry neophytes too.*

If your contact grill has more than one temperature setting, set it to high for this recipe.

## Tip

Tamarind fruit is native to Asia and North Africa and grows extensively in India. The pods are full of tiny seeds and a sweet-sour pulp that is used frequently in Indian cooking. Tamarind paste can be found in East Indian and Asian markets.

## Make Ahead

Prepare burgers up to 8 hours in advance. Wrap tightly in plastic wrap and refrigerate until ready to grill.

• **Preheat contact grill**

| | | |
|---|---|---|
| 1 lb | lean ground beef | 500 g |
| 2 | cloves garlic, minced | 2 |
| 1 | egg, beaten | 1 |
| ¼ cup | dry bread crumbs | 50 mL |
| 2 tbsp | chopped fresh cilantro | 25 mL |
| 1 tbsp | dried onion flakes | 15 mL |
| 2 tsp | curry powder | 10 mL |
| 1 tsp | tamarind paste | 5 mL |
| ½ tsp | powdered turmeric | 2 mL |
| ½ tsp | cumin seeds | 2 mL |
| ¼ tsp | kosher salt | 1 mL |
| ¼ tsp | hot pepper flakes | 1 mL |
| 6 | pieces naan bread | 6 |
| | Mango chutney (optional) | |
| | Plain yogurt (optional) | |

1. In a large bowl, combine beef, garlic, egg, bread crumbs, cilantro, onion flakes, curry powder, tamarind paste, turmeric, cumin, salt and hot pepper flakes. Mix well. Shape into 6 patties ½ inch (1 cm) thick.

2. Spray both sides of contact grill with vegetable cooking spray or oil. Place patties on grill, close lid and grill for 5 to 7 minutes, or until no longer pink and internal temperature has reached 160°F (71°C).

3. Wrap burgers in naan bread and serve topped with mango chutney and/or plain yogurt, if using.

### Variation
Use half ground pork and half ground beef in place of all ground beef.

# Thai Curry Burgers

**MAKES
6 BURGERS**

*Curry in a hurry with these terrific Thai burgers. Top with sliced fresh mango for a magnificent meal.*

If your contact grill has more than one temperature setting, set it to high for this recipe.

## Tips

Coarser than other bread crumbs, panko crumbs make for a wonderfully crunchy crust. They can be purchased in Asian markets.

Green Thai curry paste is rich in flavor and varies in heat level. Check labels to determine the spiciness.

Leftover coconut milk can be frozen in an airtight container for another use.

## Make Ahead

Prepare burgers up to 8 hours in advance. Wrap tightly in plastic wrap and refrigerate until ready to grill.

• **Preheat contact grill**

| | | |
|---|---|---|
| 1 lb | lean ground beef | 500 g |
| 2 | cloves garlic, minced | 2 |
| 1 | egg, beaten | 1 |
| 1 | stalk lemongrass (white part only), minced | 1 |
| 1/3 cup | dried panko crumbs | 75 mL |
| 1 tbsp | dried onion flakes | 15 mL |
| 1 tbsp | chopped fresh basil (or 1 tsp/5 mL dried) | 15 mL |
| 1 tbsp | green Thai curry paste | 15 mL |
| 1 tbsp | coconut milk | 15 mL |
| 1/2 tsp | ground coriander | 2 mL |
| 1/2 tsp | kosher salt | 2 mL |
| 1/4 tsp | freshly ground black pepper | 1 mL |
| 6 | whole wheat buns | 6 |

1. In a large bowl, combine beef, garlic, egg, lemongrass, panko crumbs, onion flakes, basil, curry paste, coconut milk, coriander, salt and pepper. Shape into 6 patties 1/2 inch (1 cm) thick.

2. Spray both sides of contact grill with vegetable cooking spray or oil. Place patties on grill, close lid and grill for 5 to 7 minutes, or until no longer pink and internal temperature has reached 160°F (71°C).

3. Serve in whole wheat buns.

### Variation
Use an equal amount of ground chicken or turkey in place of ground beef and grill for 6 to 8 minutes, to an internal temperature of 175°F (80°C).

# Burgers with Horseradish and Caramelized Onions

*Creamy horseradish gives these burgers a flair. Pair with caramelized onions for a real treat.*

If your contact grill has more than one temperature setting, set it to high for this recipe.

**Make Ahead**

Prepare burgers up to 8 hours in advance. Wrap tightly in plastic wrap and refrigerate until ready to grill.

• Preheat contact grill

| | | |
|---|---|---|
| 1 lb | lean ground beef | 500 g |
| 2 | cloves garlic, minced | 2 |
| 1 | shallot, finely minced (about ¼ cup/50 mL) | 1 |
| 1 | egg, beaten | 1 |
| ½ cup | dry bread crumbs | 125 mL |
| 1 tbsp | prepared horseradish | 15 mL |
| 1 tbsp | grainy mustard | 15 mL |
| ½ tsp | kosher salt | 2 mL |
| ¼ tsp | freshly ground black pepper | 1 mL |
| 6 | crusty white buns | 6 |
| | Caramelized Onions (see recipe, right) | |

1. In a large bowl, combine beef, garlic, shallot, egg, bread crumbs, horseradish, mustard, salt and pepper. Shape into 6 patties ½ inch (1 cm) thick.
2. Spray both sides of contact grill with vegetable cooking spray or oil. Place patties on grill, close lid and grill for 5 to 7 minutes, or until no longer pink and internal temperature has reached 160°F (71°C).
3. Top with Caramelized Onions (see recipe, opposite). Serve in crusty white buns.

**Variation**

Use an equal amount of ground chicken or turkey in place of ground beef and grill 6 to 8 minutes, to an internal temperature of 175°F (80°C).

# Caramelized Onions

**Tip**
Use sweet Vidalia
onions from Vidalia,
Georgia, if possible.
They produce the most
delectable caramelized
onions because of their
delicate sweetness.

| 1 | large onion, thinly sliced | 1 |
|---|---|---|
| 1 tbsp | butter | 15 mL |
| 1 tbsp | granulated sugar | 15 mL |
| 1 tbsp | balsamic vinegar | 15 mL |

1. In a nonstick skillet set over low heat, sauté onions in butter until translucent, about 8 minutes.

2. Sprinkle sugar over onions, cover and cook over low heat for another 8 minutes.

3. Sprinkle balsamic vinegar over onions, uncover and cook, stirring frequently, for about 2 minutes, or until onions are caramelized.

**Variation**
In place of balsamic vinegar, use the same amount of cooking sherry.

# Italian Veal Burgers

**MAKES
6 BURGERS**

*Grainy mustard is a must
for this savory burger that
showcases ground veal.*

If your contact grill
has more than one
temperature setting,
set it to high for
this recipe.

**Tip**
Add 1 tbsp (15 mL) more
dry bread crumbs if the
mixture is too moist.

**Make Ahead**
Prepare burgers up
to 8 hours in advance.
Wrap tightly in plastic
wrap and refrigerate
until ready to grill.

• **Preheat contact grill**

| 1 lb | ground veal | 500 g |
| 2 | cloves garlic, minced | 2 |
| 1 | egg, beaten | 1 |
| 1/3 cup | dry bread crumbs | 75 mL |
| 2 tbsp | minced green onion | 25 mL |
| 2 tbsp | grainy mustard | 25 mL |
| 1 tbsp | creamy horseradish sauce | 15 mL |
| 1 tsp | dried Italian seasoning | 5 mL |
| 1/2 tsp | kosher salt | 2 mL |
| 1/4 tsp | freshly ground black pepper | 1 mL |
| 6 | crusty Italian buns | 6 |

**1.** In a large bowl, combine veal, garlic, egg, bread crumbs, green onion, mustard, horseradish, Italian seasoning, salt and pepper. Mix well. Shape into 6 patties 1/2 inch (1 cm) thick.

**2.** Spray both sides of contact grill with vegetable cooking spray or oil. Place patties on grill, close lid and grill for 6 to 8 minutes, or until no longer pink and internal temperature has reached 160°F (71°C).

**3.** Garnish with your favorite toppings and serve in crusty Italian buns.

**Variation**
Use half ground veal and half ground beef in place of all ground veal.

# Sausage Burgers

*Hot Italian sausage takes these burgers up a notch with a burst of spicy seasoning.*

If your contact grill has more than one temperature setting, set it to high for this recipe.

## Tips

Garnish with your favorite toppings, such as Dijon mustard, lettuce, pickles and tomatoes.

Hot Italian sausage adds great zing. If you prefer, use a milder version.

## Make Ahead

Prepare burgers up to 8 hours in advance. Wrap tightly in plastic wrap and refrigerate until ready to grill.

• **Preheat contact grill**

| | | |
|---|---|---|
| 8 oz | lean ground beef | 250 g |
| 8 oz | hot Italian sausage, removed from casings and crumbled | 250 g |
| 1 | egg | 1 |
| 1 | clove garlic, minced | 1 |
| 1/3 cup | soda cracker crumbs | 75 mL |
| 1/4 cup | barbecue sauce | 50 mL |
| 1 tbsp | dried onion flakes | 15 mL |
| 1/4 tsp | kosher salt | 1 mL |
| Pinch | freshly ground black pepper | Pinch |
| 6 | panini buns | 6 |

1. In a large bowl, combine beef, sausage, egg, garlic, cracker crumbs, barbecue sauce, onion flakes, salt and pepper. Mix well. Shape into 6 patties 1/2 inch (1 cm) thick.
2. Spray both sides of contact grill with vegetable cooking spray or oil. Place patties on grill, close lid and grill for 6 to 8 minutes, or until no longer pink and internal temperature has reached 160°F (71°C).
3. Serve in panini buns.

### Variation
Use an equal amount of ketchup in place of barbecue sauce.

# Portobello Mushroom Burgers

*Grilled portobellos are the ultimate in vegetarian cuisine and can be dressed up with grilled veggies, pesto and more.*

If your contact grill has more than one temperature setting, set it to high for this recipe.

**Tip**

Earthy, meaty portobellos can now be found in supermarkets among the other cultivated mushrooms.

**Make Ahead**

Prepare marinade up to 1 day in advance. Cover and refrigerate.

## Marinade

| | | |
|---|---|---|
| 2 | cloves garlic, minced | 2 |
| 2 tbsp | olive oil | 25 mL |
| 1 1/2 tbsp | red wine vinegar | 22 mL |
| 1 tsp | dried basil | 5 mL |
| 1/4 tsp | kosher salt | 1 mL |
| 1/4 tsp | freshly ground black pepper | 1 mL |

## Burgers

| | | |
|---|---|---|
| 4 | portobello mushrooms (about 4 inches/10 cm in diameter) | 4 |
| 1 | red bell pepper, quartered | 1 |
| 1 | red onion, quartered | 1 |
| 4 | Kaiser buns or multigrain buns | 4 |
| | Olive oil (optional) | |
| 2 tbsp | freshly grated Parmesan cheese | 25 mL |

1. In a small bowl, whisk together garlic, olive oil, vinegar, basil, salt and pepper.

2. Clean mushrooms with a brush and remove stems. Place in a shallow dish. Brush two-thirds of the marinade on the mushrooms, covering both sides. Cover and refrigerate for a minimum of 20 minutes or for up to 1 hour. Meanwhile, preheat contact grill.

**3.** Spray both sides of contact grill with vegetable cooking spray or oil. Brush remaining marinade on red pepper and onions and place them on the grill, along with the mushrooms. Close lid and grill onions for 4 to 6 minutes, mushrooms for 5 minutes, until softened and grill-marked, and pepper for 4 minutes, until softened. Transfer to a plate and keep warm.

**4.** Cut buns and brush olive oil on cut sides, if desired. Place cut-side down on grill, close lid and grill for 1 minute.

**5.** *Assemble sandwiches:* Top each mushroom with grilled vegetables and sprinkle Parmesan on top. Serve in toasted Kaisers or multigrain buns.

### Variation

In place of garlic and olive oil marinade, use ¼ cup (50 mL) prepared or homemade pesto (see recipe, page 117) for a sensational pairing. Marinate the mushrooms and other vegetables in pesto instead of marinade and follow the directions for grilling.

# Hickory Chicken Burgers

*Grilling is an excellent way to prepare lean ground chicken: the chicken stays moist thanks to the high heat and the speed of this cooking method. The addition of hickory barbecue sauce imparts a smoky essence.*

If your contact grill has more than one temperature setting, set it to high for this recipe.

## Tip
Garnish with black bean sauce and your favorite toppings, such as lettuce, tomatoes and onions.

## Make Ahead
Prepare burgers up to 8 hours in advance. Wrap tightly in plastic wrap and refrigerate until ready to grill.

• **Preheat contact grill**

| | | |
|---|---|---|
| 2 | cloves garlic, minced | 2 |
| 1 | egg, beaten | 1 |
| 1 lb | lean ground chicken | 500 g |
| ½ cup | dry bread crumbs | 125 mL |
| 2 tbsp | hickory barbecue sauce | 25 mL |
| 1 tsp | dried onion flakes | 5 mL |
| 1 tsp | liquid hickory smoke | 5 mL |
| ¼ tsp | kosher salt | 1 mL |
| ¼ tsp | freshly ground black pepper | 1 mL |
| 6 | whole wheat buns | 6 |

1. In a large bowl, combine garlic, egg, chicken, bread crumbs, hickory barbecue sauce, onion flakes, liquid hickory smoke, salt and pepper. Shape into 6 patties ½-inch (1 cm) thick.

2. Spray both sides of contact grill with vegetable cooking spray or oil. Place patties on grill, close lid and grill for 6 to 8 minutes, or until no longer pink and internal temperature has reached 175°F (80°C).

3. Serve in whole wheat buns.

### Variation
Use an equal amount of ground beef in place of ground chicken and grill for 5 to 7 minutes, to an internal temperature of 160°F (71°C).

# Tarragon Mustard Chicken Burgers

*Grainy mustard jazzes up these light-hearted, healthful chicken burgers.*

If your contact grill has more than one temperature setting, set it to high for this recipe.

## Tip
Garnish with hot pepper sauce, mayonnaise and your favorite toppings, such as sliced red onion, pickles and Swiss cheese.

## Make Ahead
Prepare burgers up to 8 hours in advance. Wrap tightly in plastic wrap and refrigerate until ready to grill.

• Preheat contact grill

| | | |
|---|---|---|
| 1 lb | lean ground chicken | 500 g |
| 2 | cloves garlic, minced | 2 |
| 1 | egg, beaten | 1 |
| 1/3 cup | dry bread crumbs | 75 mL |
| 2 tbsp | grainy mustard | 25 mL |
| 1 tbsp | dried onion flakes | 15 mL |
| 1 tsp | dried tarragon | 5 mL |
| 1/2 tsp | kosher salt | 2 mL |
| 1/4 tsp | freshly ground black pepper | 1 mL |
| 6 | whole wheat buns | 6 |

1. In a large bowl, combine chicken, garlic, egg, bread crumbs, mustard, onion flakes, tarragon, salt and pepper. Shape into 6 patties 1/2 inch (1 cm) thick.
2. Spray both sides of contact grill with vegetable cooking spray or oil. Place patties on grill, close lid and grill for 6 to 8 minutes, or until no longer pink and internal temperature has reached 175°F (80°C).
3. Serve in whole wheat buns.

### Variation
Use an equal amount of ground beef in place of ground chicken and grill for 5 to 7 minutes, to an internal temperature of 160°F (71°C).

# Cheesy Turkey Burgers

*Freshen up a workday meal with these tasty turkey burgers.*

If your contact grill has more than one temperature setting, set it to high for this recipe.

## Tips

Garnish with mayonnaise and Dijon mustard and your favorite toppings, such as lettuce, pickles and tomatoes.

Less salt is required in this recipe due to the saltiness of the crackers and Asiago cheese.

## Make Ahead

Prepare burgers up to 8 hours in advance. Wrap tightly in plastic wrap and refrigerate until ready to grill.

• **Preheat contact grill**

| | | |
|---|---|---|
| ¼ cup | coarse buttery cracker crumbs, such as Ritz (about 7 crackers) | 50 mL |
| 2 tbsp | milk | 25 mL |
| 1 lb | lean ground turkey | 500 g |
| 1 | egg, beaten | 1 |
| 1 | clove garlic, minced | 1 |
| 2 tbsp | grated Asiago cheese | 25 mL |
| 1 tbsp | finely minced onion | 15 mL |
| ¼ tsp | kosher salt | 1 mL |
| ¼ tsp | freshly ground black pepper | 1 mL |
| 6 | multigrain buns | 6 |

1. In a large bowl, soak cracker crumbs in milk until liquid is absorbed, about 5 minutes.
2. Add turkey, egg, garlic, cheese, onion, salt and pepper to soaked cracker crumbs. Mix well. Shape into 6 patties ½ inch (1 cm) thick.
3. Spray both sides of contact grill with vegetable cooking spray or oil. Place patties on grill, close lid and grill for 6 to 8 minutes, or until no longer pink and internal temperature has reached 175°F (80°C).
4. Serve in multigrain buns.

## Variation
Use an equal amount of ground chicken in place of ground turkey.

# Creamy Turkey Burgers

*The twist in this burger recipe is the combination of cream cheese and sweet pickles. The minced green onion adds some color.*

If your contact grill has more than one temperature setting, set it to high for this recipe.

## Tips

Garnish with your favorite toppings, such as Dijon mustard, lettuce, onions and tomatoes.

Use herb-flavored cream cheese for added flavor.

## Make Ahead

Prepare burgers up to 8 hours in advance. Wrap tightly in plastic wrap and refrigerate until ready to grill.

• **Preheat contact grill**

| | | |
|---|---|---|
| 2 | cloves garlic, minced | 2 |
| 1 | egg | 1 |
| 1 | green onion, minced | 1 |
| 1 lb | lean ground turkey | 500 g |
| 1/4 cup | soda cracker crumbs | 50 mL |
| 1/4 cup | finely minced sweet gherkin pickles | 50 mL |
| 1/4 cup | cream cheese, at room temperature | 50 mL |
| 1/2 tsp | paprika | 2 mL |
| 1/4 tsp | kosher salt | 1 mL |
| 1/4 tsp | freshly ground black pepper | 1 mL |
| 6 | crusty Italian buns | 6 |

1. In a large bowl, combine garlic, egg, green onion, ground turkey, cracker crumbs, gherkins, cream cheese, paprika, salt and pepper. Mix well. Shape into 6 patties 1/2-inch (1 cm) thick.

2. Spray both sides of contact grill with vegetable cooking spray or oil. Place patties on grill, close lid and grill for 6 to 8 minutes, or until no longer pink and internal temperature has reached 175°F (80°C).

3. Serve in crusty Italian buns.

# Pimiento Turkey Burgers

**MAKES
6 BURGERS**

*This burger is bursting with color and flavor thanks to the green olives with pimiento and Dijon mayonnaise. For a change, consider serving the burgers in whole wheat pita halves.*

If your contact grill has more than one temperature setting, set it to high for this recipe.

**Tip**
Garnish with salsa, red onions, tomatoes and lettuce.

**Make Ahead**
Prepare burgers up to 8 hours in advance. Wrap tightly in plastic wrap and refrigerate until ready to grill.

• **Preheat contact grill**

| | | |
|---|---|---|
| 2 | cloves garlic, minced | 2 |
| 2 | green onions, chopped | 2 |
| 1 | egg, beaten | 1 |
| 1 lb | lean ground turkey | 500 g |
| 1/3 cup | dry bread crumbs | 75 mL |
| 1/4 cup | green olives with pimiento, chopped | 50 mL |
| 2 tbsp | Dijon mayonnaise | 25 mL |
| 1/4 tsp | kosher salt | 1 mL |
| 1/4 tsp | freshly ground black pepper | 1 mL |
| 6 | onion buns | 6 |

1. In a large bowl, combine garlic, green onions, egg, ground turkey, bread crumbs, olives, mayonnaise, salt and pepper. Mix well. Shape into 6 patties 1/2 inch (1 cm) thick.

2. Spray both sides of contact grill with vegetable cooking spray or oil. Place patties on grill, close lid and grill for 6 to 8 minutes, or until no longer pink and internal temperature has reached 175°F (80°C).

3. Serve in onion buns.

**Variation**
In place of Dijon mayonnaise, combine 1 tbsp (15 mL) each Dijon mustard and mayonnaise.

# Turkey Mango Burgers

*Mango chutney adds a delicate sweetness and flavor to this dish. For more mango punch, purée fresh ripe mango and use in place of mango chutney.*

If your contact grill has more than one temperature setting, set it to high for this recipe.

## Tips

Add 1 tbsp (15 mL) more dry bread crumbs if the mixture is too moist.

Garnish with plum sauce and sautéed onions and mushrooms.

## Make Ahead

Prepare burgers up to 8 hours in advance. Wrap tightly in plastic wrap and refrigerate until ready to grill.

• Preheat contact grill

| | | |
|---|---|---|
| 1 lb | lean ground turkey | 500 g |
| 2 | cloves garlic, minced | 2 |
| 1 | egg, beaten | 1 |
| 1/3 cup | dry bread crumbs | 75 mL |
| 1 tbsp | dried onion flakes | 15 mL |
| 2 tbsp | mango chutney (see tip, page 122) | 25 mL |
| 1 tbsp | hoisin sauce | 15 mL |
| 1/2 tsp | sesame oil | 2 mL |
| 1/4 tsp | freshly ground black pepper | 1 mL |
| 6 | white or egg buns | 6 |

1. In a large bowl, combine turkey, garlic, egg, bread crumbs, onion flakes, mango chutney, hoisin sauce, sesame oil and pepper. Mix well. Shape into 6 patties 1/2 inch (1 cm) thick.

2. Spray both sides of contact grill with vegetable cooking spray or oil. Place patties on grill, close lid and grill for 6 to 8 minutes, or until no longer pink and internal temperature has reached 175°F (80°C).

3. Serve in white or egg buns.

## Variation
Use an equal amount of ground chicken in place of ground turkey.

# Turkey Thyme Burgers

MAKES
6 BURGERS

*Lean ground turkey burgers on whole wheat buns make for an easy midweek meal.*

If your contact grill has more than one temperature setting, set it to high for this recipe.

## Tips

Garnish with cranberry sauce and your favorite toppings.

Add 1 tbsp (15 mL) more chicken stock if the mixture is too dry.

## Make Ahead

Prepare burgers up to 8 hours in advance. Wrap tightly in plastic wrap and refrigerate until ready to grill.

• **Preheat contact grill**

| | | |
|---|---|---|
| 1 lb | lean ground turkey | 500 g |
| 2 | cloves garlic, minced | 2 |
| 1 | egg, beaten | 1 |
| ¼ cup | corn flakes crumbs | 50 mL |
| 1 tbsp | chopped fresh thyme (or 1 tsp/5 mL dried) | 15 mL |
| 1 tbsp | dried onion flakes | 15 mL |
| 1 tbsp | chicken stock | 15 mL |
| 1½ tsp | chopped fresh sage (or ½ tsp/2 mL dried) | 7 mL |
| ½ tsp | kosher salt | 2 mL |
| ¼ tsp | freshly ground black pepper | 1 mL |
| 6 | onion buns | 6 |

1. In a large bowl, combine turkey, garlic, egg, corn flakes crumbs, thyme, onion flakes, chicken stock, sage, salt and pepper. Mix well. Shape into 6 patties ½ inch (1 cm) thick.

2. Spray both sides of contact grill with vegetable cooking spray or oil. Place patties on grill, close lid and grill for 6 to 8 minutes, or until no longer pink and internal temperature has reached 175°F (80°C).

3. Serve in onion buns.

### Variation
Use an equal amount of ground chicken in place of ground turkey.

# Main Entrées: Beef

Hot and Smoky Beef . . . . . . . . . . . . . . . . . . . . . . . . . . . . . 90

Beer-Basted Beef . . . . . . . . . . . . . . . . . . . . . . . . . . . . . . . 91

Beef Souvlaki . . . . . . . . . . . . . . . . . . . . . . . . . . . . . . . . . . 92

Steak and Vegetable "Stir-Fry" . . . . . . . . . . . . . . . . . . . . 94

Barbecued Steak . . . . . . . . . . . . . . . . . . . . . . . . . . . . . . . 96

Mustard-Infused Steak . . . . . . . . . . . . . . . . . . . . . . . . . . 97

Fajitas . . . . . . . . . . . . . . . . . . . . . . . . . . . . . . . . . . . . . . . 98

Pita Fajitas . . . . . . . . . . . . . . . . . . . . . . . . . . . . . . . . . . . 100

Pepper Steak . . . . . . . . . . . . . . . . . . . . . . . . . . . . . . . . . 102

Mexican Steak . . . . . . . . . . . . . . . . . . . . . . . . . . . . . . . . 103

Grilled Salisbury Steak . . . . . . . . . . . . . . . . . . . . . . . . . 104

Moroccan Steak . . . . . . . . . . . . . . . . . . . . . . . . . . . . . . 106

# Hot and Smoky Beef

*You can replicate the smokiness of outdoor grilling in no time with this recipe.*

If your contact grill has more than one temperature setting, set it to high for this recipe.

**Tip**
Omit the cumin if you prefer a less spiced steak.

| 1 tbsp | hot chili garlic sauce | 20 mL |
|--------|------------------------|-------|
| 2 tsp | chili powder | 10 mL |
| 1 tsp | paprika | 5 mL |
| 1 tsp | liquid smoke, divided | 5 mL |
| ½ tsp | ground cumin | 2 mL |
| ½ tsp | freshly ground black pepper | 2 mL |
| 1 lb | top sirloin steak | 500 g |

1. In a small bowl, stir together chili garlic sauce, chili powder, paprika, ½ tsp (2 mL) of the liquid smoke, cumin and pepper.

2. On a cutting board, sprinkle the remaining ¼ tsp (1 mL) liquid smoke on each side of steak. Cover with plastic wrap, and pound meat until ½ inch (1 cm) thick. Place in a shallow dish. Brush marinade on both sides of steak, coating evenly. Cover and refrigerate for a minimum of 20 minutes or for up to 1 day. Meanwhile, preheat contact grill.

3. Spray both sides of contact grill with vegetable cooking spray or oil. Place steak on grill, close lid and grill for 3 to 6 minutes, or until steak reaches an internal temperature of 160°F (71°C) for medium or 170°F (75°C) for well done.

**Variation**
Use strip loin steak in place of top sirloin.

# Beer-Basted Beef

*This melt-in-your mouth beef is tender and tasty, thanks to the beer and the lime juice.*

If your contact grill has more than one temperature setting, set it to high for this recipe.

**Tip**

For a spicier version, add a few drops of hot pepper sauce to marinade.

| | | |
|---|---|---|
| 2 | garlic cloves, minced | 2 |
| 1/2 cup | dark beer | 125 mL |
| 1 tsp | granulated sugar | 5 mL |
| 1 tsp | Worcestershire sauce | 5 mL |
| 1/2 tsp | kosher salt | 2 mL |
| 1/4 tsp | freshly ground black pepper | 1 mL |
| | Juice of 1/2 lime | |
| 1 lb | top sirloin steak | 500 g |

1. In a microwave-safe measuring cup or bowl, stir together garlic, beer, sugar, Worcestershire sauce, salt, pepper and lime juice. Microwave on Low (10%) for 2 minutes, until sugar is dissolved. Stir at the halfway point. Let cool.

2. On a cutting board, pound meat until 1/2 inch (1 cm) thick. Place in a shallow dish. Brush marinade on both sides of steak, coating evenly. Cover and refrigerate for a minimum of 20 minutes or for up to 1 day. Meanwhile, preheat contact grill.

3. Spray both sides of contact grill with vegetable cooking spray or oil. Place steak on grill, close lid and grill for 3 to 6 minutes, or until steak reaches an internal temperature of 160°F (71°C) for medium or 170°F (75°C) for well done.

**Variations**

Use strip loin steak in place of top sirloin.

For a non-alcoholic variation, replace the dark beer with root beer and omit the sugar. Root beer works well as a tenderizer!

# Beef Souvlaki

SERVES 4

*Skewered marinated meat is a breeze on the grill and lends itself to advance preparation. Serve this Greek-inspired dish with Tzatziki Sauce (see recipe opposite) and Greek salad.*

If your contact grill has more than one temperature setting, set it to high for this recipe.

• **Eight 9-inch (23 cm) bamboo skewers**

| | | |
|---|---|---|
| 2 | cloves garlic, minced | 2 |
| 1 tbsp | chopped fresh oregano (or 1 tsp/5 mL dried oregano leaves) | 15 mL |
| 1 tbsp | olive oil | 15 mL |
| 2 tsp | freshly squeezed lemon juice | 10 mL |
| ½ tsp | kosher salt | 2 mL |
| ¼ tsp | freshly ground black pepper | 1 mL |
| 1 lb | top sirloin steak, cut into 1-inch (2.5 cm) cubes | 500 g |
| 8 | Greek pitas | 8 |
| 4 | small tomatoes, quartered | 4 |
| 1 | red onion, quartered | 1 |

**1.** Soak bamboo skewers in hot water for 30 minutes.

**2.** In a small bowl, whisk together garlic, oregano, olive oil, lemon juice, salt and pepper.

**3.** Thread cubes of beef on soaked bamboo skewers and place in a shallow dish. Brush marinade on steak, coating evenly. Cover and refrigerate for a minimum of 20 minutes or for up to 1 day. Meanwhile, preheat contact grill.

**4.** Spray both sides of contact grill with vegetable cooking spray or oil. Separate onion quarters into slices, place on grill, close lid and grill for 4 minutes. Place tomato quarters on grill, close lid and grill for 1 minute. Transfer to a bowl, cover and keep warm.

**5.** Place skewers on grill, close lid and grill for 5 to 6 minutes, or until steak reaches an internal temperature of 160°F (71°C) for medium or 170°F (75°C) for well done.

**6.** Reduce grill to medium heat, if possible. Just before serving, place pitas on grill and, with lid open, heat pitas for 1 minute.

**7.** Remove meat from skewers. On each pita, place meat, tomatoes and onion. Roll up.

# Tzatziki Sauce

**MAKES 1½ CUPS (375 ML)**

**Tip**

If you don't have cheesecloth on hand, use a basket paper coffee filter in its place, setting it over the colander.

| | | |
|---|---|---|
| 1 cup | plain yogurt | 250 mL |
| ½ | English cucumber, peeled and diced | ½ |
| 2 | cloves garlic, minced | 2 |
| 2 tbsp | freshly squeezed lemon juice | 25 mL |
| 1 tbsp | chopped fresh dill | 15 mL |
| ¼ tsp | salt | 1 mL |
| ¼ tsp | freshly ground black pepper | 1 mL |

1. Place yogurt in a cheesecloth-lined colander and place colander over a bowl. Cover, refrigerate and let drain overnight to thicken. Discard liquid.

2. In a medium bowl, combine thickened yogurt with cucumber, lemon juice, dill, salt and pepper. Stir well, cover and refrigerate for a minimum of 1 to 2 hours or for up to 1 day before serving.

# Steak and Vegetable "Stir-Fry"

**SERVES 4**

*If you crave stir-fry without heaps of added fat, you'll appreciate this sensational recipe for its savory taste and low-fat flare.*

If your contact grill has more than one temperature setting, set it to high for this recipe.

**Tip**

Chinese five-spice powder usually includes anise, cinnamon, cloves, Szechuan pepper and ground ginger and can be found in well-stocked supermarkets and bulk-food stores.

| | | |
|---|---|---|
| 2 | cloves garlic, minced | 2 |
| 3 tbsp | soy sauce | 45 mL |
| 3 tbsp | seasoned rice vinegar | 45 mL |
| 2 tbsp | hoisin sauce | 25 mL |
| 1½ tsp | minced gingerroot | 7 mL |
| Pinch | Chinese five-spice powder | Pinch |
| 1 lb | top sirloin steak, cut across the grain into 1- by ¼-inch (2.5 by 0.5 cm) slices | 500 g |
| 2 cups | broccoli florets (about 8 oz/250 g) | 500 mL |
| ½ | red bell pepper | ½ |
| ½ | green bell pepper | ½ |
| 1 | small onion, quartered | 1 |
| 1 cup | snow peas | 250 mL |
| 1 cup | halved mushrooms | 250 mL |

1. In a small bowl, whisk together garlic, soy sauce, rice vinegar, hoisin sauce, gingerroot and five-spice powder.

2. Place steak pieces in a shallow dish. Brush ⅓ cup (75 mL) marinade on steak, turning several times to coat both sides evenly. Cover and refrigerate for a minimum of 20 minutes or for up to 1 day. Meanwhile, preheat contact grill.

3. Place broccoli in a shallow dish and brush with 1 tbsp (15 mL) marinade. Toss to coat. Place on grill, close lid and grill for 10 minutes, or until tender-crisp. Transfer to a serving bowl, cover and keep warm.

4. Place onions and red and green peppers in the shallow dish and brush with 1 tbsp (15 mL) marinade. Toss to coat. Separate onion quarters into layers. Place on grill, close lid and grill for 4 to 6 minutes. Transfer to the serving bowl, cover and keep warm.

5. Place peppers on grill. Close lid and grill for 4 minutes. Transfer to the serving bowl, cover and keep warm.

6. Place mushroom halves in the shallow dish and brush with $1\frac{1}{2}$ tsp (7 mL) marinade. Toss to coat. Place on grill, close lid and grill for 3 minutes. Transfer to the serving bowl, cover and keep warm.

7. Place snow peas in the shallow dish and brush with $1\frac{1}{2}$ tsp (7 m L) marinade. Toss to coat. Place on grill, close lid and grill for 2 minutes. Transfer to the serving bowl, cover and keep warm.

8. Spray both sides of contact grill with vegetable cooking spray or oil. Place steak pieces on grill, close lid and grill for 3 to 5 minutes, or until steak is desired doneness.

9. Meanwhile, slice the red and green peppers and return them to the serving bowl.

**Variation**
Use strip loin steak in place of top sirloin.

# Barbecued Steak

*This barbecue-influenced grilled steak imparts the flavor of outdoor barbecuing in the comfort of your home.*

If your contact grill has more than one temperature setting, set it to high for this recipe.

**Tip**

Omit the cayenne if you prefer a less spiced steak.

| | | |
|---|---|---|
| 1¹/₂ tbsp | packed brown sugar | 22 mL |
| 2 tsp | sweet paprika | 10 mL |
| 1 tsp | dry mustard powder | 5 mL |
| ¹/₂ tsp | kosher salt | 2 mL |
| ¹/₂ tsp | freshly ground black pepper | 2 mL |
| Pinch | cayenne pepper | Pinch |
| 1 lb | top sirloin steak | 500 g |

1. In a small bowl, stir together brown sugar, paprika, mustard powder, salt, pepper and cayenne.

2. Place steak on a cutting board and sprinkle half of the dry rub on one side of steak. Cover with plastic wrap and pound meat until ¹/₂ inch (1 cm) thick. Flip steak over, sprinkle on remainder of dry rub, cover with plastic wrap and pound meat to incorporate seasonings. Place in a shallow dish, cover and refrigerate for a minimum of 20 minutes or for up to 1 day. Meanwhile, preheat contact grill.

3. Spray both sides of contact grill with vegetable cooking spray or oil. Place steak on grill, close lid and grill for 3 to 6 minutes, or until steak reaches an internal temperature of 160°F (71°C) for medium or 170°F (75°C) for well done.

**Variation**
Use strip loin steak in place of top sirloin.

Chicken Nuggets (page 112)
*Overleaf:* Grilled Cheese and Asparagus Rolls (page 52)

# Mustard-Infused Steak

SERVES 4

*Grainy mustard is a must to reach the full flavor potential of this recipe.*

If your contact grill has more than one temperature setting, set it to high for this recipe.

**Tip**
Creamy horseradish is a superb condiment to have on hand; it shines in this recipe.

| | | |
|---|---|---|
| ½ cup | beer | 125 mL |
| 1½ tbsp | packed brown sugar | 22 mL |
| 1 tbsp | Worcestershire sauce | 15 mL |
| 1 tbsp | grainy mustard | 15 mL |
| 1 tbsp | creamy horseradish sauce | 15 mL |
| ½ tsp | kosher salt | 2 mL |
| ¼ tsp | freshly ground black pepper | 1 mL |
| 1 lb | top sirloin steak | 500 g |

1. In a small bowl, stir together beer, brown sugar, Worcestershire sauce, mustard, horseradish, salt and pepper.

2. Place steak on a cutting board and sprinkle half of the marinade on one side of steak. Cover with plastic wrap and pound meat until ½ inch (1 cm) thick. Flip steak over, sprinkle remainder of marinade on steak, cover with plastic wrap and pound meat to incorporate seasonings. Cover and refrigerate for a minimum of 20 minutes or for up to 1 day. Meanwhile, preheat contact grill.

3. Spray both sides of contact grill with vegetable cooking spray or oil. Place steak on grill, close lid and grill for 3 to 6 minutes, or until steak reaches an internal temperature of 160°F (71°C) for medium or 170°F (75°C) for well done.

**Variation**
Use strip loin steak in place of top sirloin.

Blackened Red Fish
(page 134)

# Fajitas

*Flour tortillas provide the perfect canvas for inspired grill cuisine. Grill vegetables of your choice, and top the meat and vegetables with sour cream, shredded Cheddar or Monterey Jack cheese, guacamole and salsa.*

If your contact grill has more than one temperature setting, set it to high for this recipe.

**Tip**
Serve with tortilla chips and salsa.

| | | |
|---|---|---|
| 2 | cloves garlic, minced | 2 |
| 3 tbsp | prepared chili sauce | 45 mL |
| 2 tsp | freshly squeezed lime juice | 10 mL |
| 1/2 tsp | ground cumin | 2 mL |
| 1/2 tsp | ground coriander | 2 mL |
| 1/2 tsp | kosher salt | 2 mL |
| 1/4 tsp | freshly ground black pepper | 1 mL |
| 1 lb | top sirloin steak, cut across the grain into 1- by 1/4-inch (2.5 by 0.5 cm) slices | 500 g |
| 8 | 10-inch (25 cm) flour tortillas | 8 |
| 1 | small onion, quartered | 1 |
| 1/2 | green bell pepper | 1/2 |
| 1/2 | red bell pepper | 1/2 |
| 1 cup | halved mushrooms | 250 mL |

**1.** In a small bowl, whisk together garlic, chili sauce, lime juice, cumin, coriander, salt and pepper.

**2.** Place steak pieces in a shallow dish. Brush marinade on steak, coating evenly. Cover and refrigerate for a minimum of 20 minutes or for up to 1 day. Meanwhile, preheat contact grill.

**3.** Spray both sides of contact grill with vegetable cooking spray or oil. Separate onion quarters into layers. Place on grill, close lid and grill for 4 to 6 minutes. Transfer to a heated serving plate, cover and keep warm.

**4.** Place green and red pepper halves on grill. Close lid and grill for 4 minutes. Transfer to the serving plate, cover and keep warm.

5. Place mushrooms on grill, close lid and grill for 3 minutes. Transfer to the serving plate with the onions and peppers, cover and keep warm.

6. Place steak pieces on grill, close lid and grill for 3 to 5 minutes, or until steak is desired doneness.

7. Meanwhile, slice onions, peppers and mushrooms. Place on heated serving plate, cover and keep warm.

8. When steak is cooked, place on heated serving plate, cover and keep warm.

9. Reduce heat to medium, if possible. Place tortillas on grill. With lid open, grill each tortilla for about 1 minute, until heated.

10. Serve buffet style, with each person filling one tortilla at a time with meat, vegetables and toppings, then rolling.

### Variation
Use an equal amount of chicken or turkey strips in place of beef and cook for 6 minutes, or until no longer pink inside.

# Pita Fajitas

SERVES 4

*This twist on the traditional tortilla fajitas offers a great coupling of chipotle-spiked steak and pita, along with grilled vegetables. It is still simple, fast and nutritious. Serve with guacamole, sour cream, grated Cheddar or Monterey Jack cheese and salsa.*

If your contact grill has more than one temperature setting, set it to high for this recipe.

| | | |
|---|---|---|
| 2 | cloves garlic, minced | 2 |
| 2 tbsp | freshly squeezed lime juice | 25 mL |
| 1 tbsp | minced chipotle chili peppers in adobo (see tip, page 73) | 15 mL |
| 1 tsp | chili powder | 5 mL |
| 1/2 tsp | dried oregano | 2 mL |
| 1/4 tsp | kosher salt | 1 mL |
| 1/4 tsp | freshly ground black pepper | 1 mL |
| 1 lb | top sirloin steak, cut across the grain into 1- by 1/4-inch (2.5 by 0.5 cm) slices | 500 g |
| 1 | small onion, quartered | 1 |
| 1/2 | green bell pepper | 1/2 |
| 1/2 | red bell pepper | 1/2 |
| 1 cup | halved mushrooms | 250 mL |
| 4 | pitas | 4 |

1. In a small bowl, whisk together garlic, lime juice, chilies, chili powder, oregano, salt and pepper.

2. Place steak pieces in a shallow dish. Brush marinade on steak, coating evenly. Cover and refrigerate for a minimum of 20 minutes or for up to 1 day. Meanwhile, preheat contact grill.

3. Spray both sides of contact grill with vegetable cooking spray or oil. Separate onion quarters into layers. Place on grill, close lid and grill for 4 to 6 minutes. Transfer to a heated serving plate, cover and keep warm.

4. Place green and red pepper halves on grill. Close lid and grill for 4 minutes. Transfer to the serving plate, cover and keep warm.

5. Place mushrooms on grill, close lid and grill for 3 minutes. Add to the serving plate, cover and keep warm.

6. Place steak pieces on grill, close lid and grill for 3 to 5 minutes, or until steak is desired doneness.

7. Meanwhile, slice onions, peppers and mushrooms. Place on heated serving plate, cover and keep warm.

8. When steak is cooked, place on heated serving plate, cover and keep warm.

9. Slice pita breads in half crosswise and carefully open to create pockets. Reduce grill heat to medium, if possible. Place pitas on grill and, with lid open, heat for 1 minute.

10. Serve buffet style, with each person filling half a pita at a time with meat, vegetables and toppings.

### Variation
Add 2 tbsp (25 mL) chopped fresh cilantro to marinade.

# Pepper Steak

**SERVES 4**

*This version of pepper steak "without all the fuss" is a gastronomic delight.*

If your contact grill has more than one temperature setting, set it to high for this recipe.

**Tip**
Green peppercorns are much milder than black peppercorns and are generally sold in jars or cans packed in brine. Look for them in specialty food stores and well-stocked supermarkets.

| 2 | cloves garlic, minced | 2 |
|---|---|---|
| ¼ cup | dry red wine (such as merlot) | 50 mL |
| 1 tbsp | Dijon mustard | 15 mL |
| ½ tsp | kosher salt | 2 mL |
| ½ tsp | dried thyme | 2 mL |
| 2 tsp | drained green peppercorns | 10 mL |
| 1 lb | top sirloin steak | 500 g |

1. In a small bowl, whisk together garlic, wine, mustard, salt and thyme.

2. Using pestle and mortar, grind peppercorns. Add peppercorns to red wine marinade.

3. Place steak on a cutting board and sprinkle half of the marinade on one side of steak. Cover with plastic wrap and pound meat until ½ inch (1 cm) thick. Flip steak over, sprinkle remainder of marinade on steak, cover with plastic wrap and pound meat to incorporate seasonings. Place in a shallow dish, cover and refrigerate for a minimum of 20 minutes or for up to 1 day. Meanwhile, preheat contact grill.

4. Spray both sides of contact grill with vegetable cooking spray or oil. Place steak on grill, close lid and grill for 3 to 6 minutes, or until steak reaches an internal temperature of 160°F (71°C) for medium or 170°F (75°C) for well done.

**Variation**
Use strip loin steak in place of top sirloin.

# Mexican Steak

SERVES 4

*Mexican cuisine is admired and is frequently created in the home kitchen. Serve this spicy dish with Mexican rice and corn.*

If your contact grill has more than one temperature setting, set it to high for this recipe.

| | | |
|---|---|---|
| 2 | cloves garlic, minced | 2 |
| 2 tbsp | chopped fresh cilantro | 25 mL |
| 1 tbsp | freshly squeezed lime juice | 15 mL |
| 2 tsp | chili powder | 10 mL |
| 1 tsp | cumin seeds | 5 mL |
| 1 tsp | minced jalapeño pepper | 5 mL |
| 1/2 tsp | kosher salt | 2 mL |
| 1/4 tsp | freshly ground black pepper | 1 mL |
| 1 lb | top sirloin steak | 500 g |

1. In a small bowl, whisk together garlic, cilantro, lime juice, cumin, chili powder, jalapeño, salt and pepper.

2. Place steak on a cutting board and sprinkle half of the marinade on one side of steak. Cover with plastic wrap and pound until 1/2 inch (1 cm) thick. Flip steak over, sprinkle remainder of marinade on steak, cover with plastic wrap and pound to incorporate seasonings. Cover and refrigerate for a minimum of 20 minutes or for up to 1 day. Meanwhile, preheat contact grill.

3. Spray both sides of contact grill with vegetable cooking spray or oil. Place steak on grill, close lid and grill for 3 to 6 minutes, or until steak reaches an internal temperature of 160°F (71°C) for medium or 170°F (75°C) for well done.

### Variation
Use an equal amount of pork tenderloin, split in half lengthwise, in place of beef. Grill for 8 minutes, or until cooked to an internal temperature of 160°F (71°C.)

# Grilled Salisbury Steak

*This dressed up "hamburger steak" is much more than a burger. It's flavor-packed and first-rate when made with ground sirloin and topped with a mushroom-onion gravy.*

If your contact grill has more than one temperature setting, set it to high for this recipe.

**Tip**

Ground sirloin is a must for this recipe rather than regular ground round or other ground beef cuts.

| | | |
|---|---|---|
| 1 tsp | olive oil | 5 mL |
| 2 | cloves garlic, minced | 2 |
| 1 | shallot, sliced thinly (about $\frac{1}{4}$ cup/50 mL) | 1 |
| $\frac{1}{2}$ cup | chopped mushrooms | 125 mL |
| 1 tbsp | Worcestershire sauce | 15 mL |
| $\frac{1}{3}$ cup | fresh bread crumbs | 75 mL |
| 3 tbsp | milk | 45 mL |
| 1 | egg, beaten | 1 |
| 1 lb | lean ground sirloin | 500 g |
| $\frac{1}{2}$ tsp | dry mustard powder | 2 mL |
| $\frac{1}{2}$ tsp | kosher salt | 2 mL |
| $\frac{1}{4}$ tsp | freshly ground black pepper | 1 mL |

**Mushroom and Onion Gravy**

| | | |
|---|---|---|
| 1 tsp | vegetable or olive oil | 5 mL |
| 1 | onion, thinly sliced | 1 |
| 1 cup | mushrooms, sliced | 250 mL |
| 1 | package (1 oz/25 g) brown gravy, prepared according to directions | 1 |

1. In a nonstick skillet, heat oil over medium-low heat. Sauté garlic, shallot and chopped mushrooms for 3 minutes, until softened. Add Worcestershire and sauté for another 2 minutes, until liquid has evaporated.

2. Meanwhile, in a large bowl, soak bread crumbs in milk until liquid is absorbed, about 5 minutes.

3. Add ground sirloin to bowl with sautéed vegetables, egg, dry mustard powder, salt and pepper. Mix well and divide into 4 patties. Flatten patties and form into oblong shapes, about $\frac{1}{2}$ inch (1 cm) thick. Place on a plate, cover and refrigerate for a minimum of 20 minutes or for up to 1 day. Meanwhile, preheat contact grill.

**4.** Spray both sides of contact grill with vegetable cooking spray or oil. Place steaks on grill, close lid and grill for 6 to 7 minutes, or until steaks are no longer pink and reach an internal temperature of 160°F (71°C).

**5.** *Prepare gravy:* In a nonstick skillet, heat oil over medium heat. Sauté onion and sliced mushrooms for about 6 minutes, until onions are golden brown. Add prepared gravy to skillet. Stir well.

**6.** Top each steak with mushroom and onion gravy.

### Variation
Use about 1¼ cups (300 mL) homemade gravy in place of the packaged version.

# Moroccan Steak

**SERVES 4**

*Serve this dish with couscous instead of potatoes and graciously accept the rave reviews.*

If your contact grill has more than one temperature setting, set it to high for this recipe.

**Tip**

Omit the hot pepper flakes if you prefer a less spiced steak.

| | | |
|---|---|---|
| 1 tbsp | dried onion flakes | 15 mL |
| 1 tbsp | dried parsley flakes | 15 mL |
| 1 tsp | powdered turmeric | 5 mL |
| 1 tsp | cumin seeds | 5 mL |
| ½ tsp | kosher salt | 2 mL |
| ¼ tsp | freshly ground black pepper | 1 mL |
| ¼ tsp | hot pepper flakes (optional) | 1 mL |
| ¼ tsp | ground cinnamon | 1 mL |
| ¼ tsp | ground ginger | 1 mL |
| Pinch | ground cloves | Pinch |
| 1 lb | top sirloin steak | 500 g |

1. In a small bowl, stir together onion flakes, parsley flakes, turmeric, cumin, salt, pepper, hot pepper flakes (if using), cinnamon, ginger and cloves.

2. Place steak on a cutting board and sprinkle half of the dry rub on one side of steak. Cover with plastic wrap and pound meat until ½ inch (1 cm) thick. Flip steak over, sprinkle on remainder of dry rub, cover with plastic wrap and pound meat to incorporate seasonings. Place in a shallow dish, cover and refrigerate for a minimum of 20 minutes or for up to 1 day. Meanwhile, preheat contact grill.

3. Spray both sides of contact grill with vegetable cooking spray or oil. Place steak on grill, close lid and grill for 3 to 6 minutes, or until steak reaches an internal temperature of 160°F (71°C) for medium or 170°F (75°C) for well done.

**Variation**
Use strip loin steak in place of top sirloin.

# Main Entrées: Chicken and Turkey

Barbecued Chicken with a Difference . . . . . . . . . . . . 108

Weekday Barbecued Chicken . . . . . . . . . . . . . . . . . . . 109

Jerk Chicken . . . . . . . . . . . . . . . . . . . . . . . . . . . . . . 110

Southern "Fried" Chicken . . . . . . . . . . . . . . . . . . . . 111

Chicken Nuggets . . . . . . . . . . . . . . . . . . . . . . . . . . 112

Chicken and Bean Burritos. . . . . . . . . . . . . . . . . . . . 114

Greek Lemon Chicken . . . . . . . . . . . . . . . . . . . . . . . 115

Pesto Chicken Thighs. . . . . . . . . . . . . . . . . . . . . . . . 116

Grilled Chicken Cacciatore . . . . . . . . . . . . . . . . . . . 118

Four-Ingredient Chicken . . . . . . . . . . . . . . . . . . . . . 120

Cayenne Raspberry Chicken . . . . . . . . . . . . . . . . . . 121

Mango Chicken . . . . . . . . . . . . . . . . . . . . . . . . . . . . 122

Coconut Mango Chicken Breasts. . . . . . . . . . . . . . . . 123

Cilantro Lime Chicken. . . . . . . . . . . . . . . . . . . . . . . . 124

Ginger, Soy and Lime Chicken. . . . . . . . . . . . . . . . . 125

Orange Sesame Chicken. . . . . . . . . . . . . . . . . . . . . . 126

Szechuan Chicken . . . . . . . . . . . . . . . . . . . . . . . . . . 128

Sticky Sesame Chicken. . . . . . . . . . . . . . . . . . . . . . . 129

Teriyaki Chicken. . . . . . . . . . . . . . . . . . . . . . . . . . . . 130

Green Peppercorn and Gruyère Turkey Fillets . . . . . . . 131

Orange Rosemary Turkey Thighs . . . . . . . . . . . . . . . . 132

# Barbecued Chicken with a Difference

*This homemade spicy barbecue sauce will wow your family with its depth of flavor, and it can be used with various boneless chicken parts or cuts of beef.*

If your contact grill has more than one temperature setting, set it to high for this recipe.

## Tip

Consider this dish homemade "fast food." You'll have most of the condiments on hand already, and it's ideal for preparing on a soccer night when you're up against the clock. Serve with pasta and prepackaged salad for a wholesome dinner in under 30 minutes.

## Make Ahead

Prepare marinade up to 1 day in advance. Cover and refrigerate.

| | | |
|---|---|---|
| 2 tbsp | ketchup | 25 mL |
| 2 tbsp | prepared chili sauce | 25 mL |
| 1 tbsp | cider vinegar | 15 mL |
| 1 tsp | packed brown sugar | 5 mL |
| 1 tsp | dried onion flakes | 5 mL |
| 1 tsp | curry powder | 5 mL |
| 1/2 tsp | kosher salt | 2 mL |
| 1/4 tsp | garlic powder | 1 mL |
| 1/4 tsp | freshly ground black pepper | 1 mL |
| 4 | boneless, skinless chicken breasts | 4 |

1. In a small bowl, whisk together ketchup, chili sauce, vinegar, brown sugar, onion flakes, curry powder, salt, garlic powder and pepper.

2. Place chicken breasts in a shallow dish. Brush marinade on chicken, coating evenly. Cover and refrigerate for a minimum of 20 minutes or for up to 1 hour. Meanwhile, preheat contact grill.

3. Spray both sides of contact grill with vegetable cooking spray or oil. Place chicken on grill, close lid and grill for 5 to 6 minutes, or until chicken is no longer pink inside and reaches an internal temperature of 170°F (75°C).

### Variation

Use 8 boneless, skinless chicken thighs in place of chicken breasts. Grill for same amount of time.

# Weekday Barbecued Chicken

*This recipe is ideal for a busy weeknight when home cooking is desired but time is short. Your kids will love the crunchy texture of this lightly breaded grilled chicken dish.*

If your contact grill has more than one temperature setting, set it to high for this recipe.

**Tip**

The bacon-flavored crackers give a savory, smoky flavor to this dish. But other favorite cheese, ranch or vegetable crackers can also be used as breading in this recipe.

| | | |
|---|---|---|
| 1 | clove garlic, minced | 1 |
| ½ cup | barbecue sauce | 125 mL |
| 1 tbsp | white vinegar | 15 mL |
| 8 | boneless, skinless chicken thighs | 8 |
| ⅓ cup | bacon-flavored cracker crumbs | 150 mL |

1. In a small bowl, whisk together garlic, barbecue sauce and vinegar.

2. Brush marinade on chicken thighs and roll in cracker crumbs, coating evenly. Discard any excess marinade and crumbs. Place breaded chicken in a shallow dish, cover and refrigerate until ready to grill. Meanwhile, preheat contact grill.

3. Spray both sides of contact grill with vegetable cooking spray or oil. Place chicken on grill, close lid and grill for 6 to 7 minutes, or until juices run clear when chicken is pierced, chicken reaches an internal temperature of 170°F (75°C) and coating is crispy.

**Variation**
Use 4 boneless, skinless chicken breasts in place of chicken thighs. Grill for same amount of time.

# Jerk Chicken

*Who needs to rely on the bottled version when it's so easy to prepare your own jerk sauce?*

If your contact grill has more than one temperature setting, set it to high for this recipe.

| | | |
|---|---|---|
| 1 | clove garlic | 1 |
| $1/2$ | Scotch bonnet chili pepper | $1/2$ |
| $1/2$ | onion | $1/2$ |
| 1 tbsp | chopped gingerroot | 15 mL |
| | Juice of 1 lime | |
| 2 tbsp | fresh thyme leaves (or 2 tsp/10 mL dried) | 25 mL |
| 1 tbsp | packed dark brown sugar | 15 mL |
| 1 tsp | ground allspice | 5 mL |
| 1 tsp | ground cinnamon | 5 mL |
| $1/2$ tsp | kosher salt | 2 mL |
| 8 | boneless, skinless chicken thighs | 8 |

**1.** In a food processor, process garlic, chili pepper, onion and gingerroot until minced. Add lime juice, thyme, brown sugar, allspice, cinnamon and salt. Process with on/off pulses until smooth.

**2.** Place chicken thighs in a shallow dish. Brush paste on chicken, coating evenly. Cover and refrigerate for a minimum of 20 minutes or for up to 1 hour. Meanwhile, preheat contact grill.

**3.** Spray both sides of contact grill with vegetable cooking spray or oil. Place chicken on grill, close lid and grill for 5 to 6 minutes, or until juices run clear when chicken is pierced and chicken reaches an internal temperature of 170°F (75°C).

## Variation
Use 4 boneless, skinless chicken breasts in place of chicken thighs. Grill for same amount of time.

## Tips
Like curry, jerk seasoning varies from cook to cook. Feel free to adapt your jerk sauce to suit your tastes and your ability to tolerate hot peppers.

Scotch bonnet peppers are small but fiery. The red, orange or yellow peppers are similar in heat factor to Jamaican hot peppers, and can be found in Caribbean specialty food stores.

## Make Ahead
Prepare jerk paste up to 1 day in advance. Cover and refrigerate.

# Southern "Fried" Chicken

*My family loves this moist chicken reminiscent of fried chicken but free of all the added fat from deep frying!*

If your contact grill has more than one temperature setting, set it to high for this recipe.

### Tip
Buttermilk powder is good to have on hand. Prepare as directed to equal ⅔ cups (150 mL) and use in place of fresh buttermilk.

### Make Ahead
Prepare coating up to 1 day in advance. Cover and refrigerate.

| | | |
|---|---|---|
| ⅔ cup | buttermilk | 150 mL |
| 1 tbsp | Dijon mustard | 15 mL |
| 1 tsp | dried onion flakes | 5 mL |
| ¼ tsp | garlic salt | 1 mL |
| ¼ tsp | freshly ground black pepper, divided | 1 mL |
| 4 | boneless, skinless chicken breasts | 4 |
| ½ cup | cornmeal | 125 mL |
| 2 tbsp | freshly grated Parmesan cheese | 25 mL |
| 1½ tsp | dried Italian seasoning | 7 mL |
| ¼ tsp | cayenne pepper | 1 mL |
| ¼ tsp | kosher salt | 1 mL |

1. In a medium bowl, whisk together buttermilk, mustard, onion flakes, garlic salt and ⅛ tsp (0.5 mL) of the pepper.

2. Dip chicken breasts in buttermilk marinade, turning several times to ensure they are evenly coated. Place in a shallow dish, cover and refrigerate for a minimum of 20 minutes or for up to 1 hour. Discard excess marinade. Meanwhile, preheat contact grill.

3. In a medium bowl, mix together cornmeal, Parmesan cheese, Italian seasoning, cayenne, salt and the remaining ⅛ tsp (0.5 mL) pepper. Coat each chicken piece in cornmeal/Parmesan mixture.

4. Spray both sides of contact grill with vegetable cooking spray or oil. Place chicken on grill, close lid and grill for 6 to 7 minutes, or until juices run clear when chicken is pierced, chicken reaches an internal temperature of 170°F (75°C) and coating is crispy.

### Variation
Use 8 boneless, skinless chicken thighs in place of chicken breasts. Add 1 to 2 tbsp (15 to 25 mL) more cornmeal to coating. Grill for same amount of time.

# Chicken Nuggets

*Chicken thighs grill beautifully on the indoor grill and make for an agreeable change from the usual chicken breasts. Serve with Honey Dill Sauce or Sweet-and-Sour Sauce (see recipes opposite).*

If your contact grill has more than one temperature setting, set it to high for this recipe.

**Tip**

For a subtle tartness, dip chicken nuggets in $\frac{1}{2}$ cup (125 mL) buttermilk in place of egg yolks before coating in breading.

| | | |
|---|---|---|
| 1$\frac{1}{4}$ cups | corn flakes crumbs | 300 mL |
| $\frac{2}{3}$ cup | freshly grated Parmesan cheese | 150 mL |
| 1 tsp | dried thyme leaves | 5 mL |
| 1 tsp | dried parsley leaves | 5 mL |
| 1 tsp | garlic powder | 5 mL |
| $\frac{1}{2}$ tsp | kosher salt | 2 mL |
| $\frac{1}{2}$ tsp | freshly ground black pepper | 2 mL |
| 2 | egg yolks | 2 |
| 8 | boneless, skinless chicken thighs | 8 |

1. In a shallow dish, mix together corn flakes crumbs, Parmesan, thyme, parsley, garlic, salt and pepper. In another shallow dish, lightly beat egg yolks.
2. Cut chicken into 1-inch (2.5 cm) pieces. Dip pieces in egg yolk and then in coating. Place in a shallow dish, cover and refrigerate for 15 minutes. Discard any excess egg and crumbs. Meanwhile, preheat contact grill.
3. Spray both sides of contact grill with vegetable cooking spray or oil. Place chicken on grill, close lid and grill for 5 to 6 minutes, or until juices run clear when chicken is pierced and coating is crisp.

**Variation**
Use 4 boneless, skinless chicken breasts in place of chicken thighs. Grill for same amount of time.

# Honey Dill Sauce

**MAKES ABOUT
1 CUP (250 ML)**

| | | |
|---|---|---|
| ½ cup | sour cream | 125 mL |
| ½ cup | mayonnaise | 125 mL |
| 1½ tbsp | liquid honey | 22 mL |
| 2 tsp | dried dillweed | 10 mL |

1. In a small bowl, stir sour cream, mayonnaise, honey and dillweed, blending well. Cover and refrigerate for up to 3 days. Use for dipping chicken nuggets, Chinese-style breaded veal nuggets or jalapeño poppers.

# Sweet-and-Sour Sauce

**MAKES ABOUT
½ CUP (125 ML)**

| | | |
|---|---|---|
| ⅓ cup | pineapple juice | 75 mL |
| ¼ cup | ketchup | 50 mL |
| 2 tbsp | packed brown sugar | 25 mL |
| 1 tbsp | vinegar | 15 mL |
| 1 tbsp | freshly squeezed lemon juice | 15 mL |

1. In a small saucepan over medium-high heat, bring pineapple juice, ketchup, brown sugar, vinegar and lemon juice to a boil. Reduce to low heat and simmer for 5 minutes, or until smooth. Serve warm or at room temperature.

# Chicken and Bean Burritos

*This dish is a favorite of my son, Jesse, fourteen. It is excellent as a quick meal for busy teenagers, and can be prepared in advance and reheated when required.*

If your contact grill has more than one temperature setting, set it to high for this recipe.

## Tip

Canned refried beans are usually pinto beans that have been boiled, mashed, then fried and seasoned. They are thick and tasty, and can be found in the international or Mexican section of the supermarket.

## Make Ahead

Burritos reheat easily. Prepare as directed above. Cool, cover tightly with plastic wrap and refrigerate for up to 1 day. Reheat briefly on Medium in the microwave or on your grill (set at medium, if possible).

| | | |
|---|---|---|
| 2 | cloves garlic, minced | 2 |
| 2 | chipotle chilies in adobo sauce, minced (see tip, page 73) | 2 |
| 1 tbsp | freshly squeezed lime juice | 15 mL |
| 1/2 tsp | dried oregano leaves | 2 mL |
| 1/2 tsp | kosher salt | 2 mL |
| 1/4 tsp | freshly ground black pepper | 1 mL |
| 4 | boneless, skinless chicken breasts | 4 |
| 1 | can (14 oz/398 mL) refried beans | 1 |
| 10 | 8-inch (20 cm) tortillas | 10 |
| 1/2 cup | shredded Cheddar cheese | 125 mL |
| 1/2 cup | shredded Monterey Jack cheese (about 2 oz/60 g) | 125 mL |
| 1/4 cup | chopped fresh cilantro | 50 mL |
| 1/4 cup | chopped green onions (optional, about 2 medium) | 50 mL |
| | Salsa | |

1. In a small bowl, whisk together garlic, chilies, lime juice, oregano, salt and pepper.

2. Place chicken breasts in a shallow dish. Brush marinade on chicken, coating evenly. Cover and refrigerate for a minimum of 20 minutes or for up to 1 day. Meanwhile, preheat contact grill.

3. Spray both sides of contact grill with vegetable cooking spray or oil. Place chicken on grill, close lid and grill for 6 minutes, or until chicken is no longer pink inside and reaches an internal temperature of 170°F (75°C). Remove from grill and slice crosswise into 1-inch (2.5 cm) strips.

4. To assemble burritos, spread about 2 to 3 tbsp (25 to 45 mL) refried beans over each tortilla. Place about 5 chicken pieces down the center. Sprinkle 1 tbsp (15 mL) Cheddar cheese, 1 tbsp (15 mL) Jack cheese, 1 tsp (5 mL) cilantro and 1 tsp (5 mL) green onions (if using). Fold in sides of tortilla and roll up. Place burritos seam side down on grill, close lid and grill for 3 minutes, until heated through and tortillas are golden. Serve with salsa.

# Greek Lemon Chicken

*Fresh lemon juice stars in this Greek-inspired chicken recipe. Serve with rice and Greek salad.*

If your contact grill has more than one temperature setting, set it to high for this recipe.

**Make Ahead**

Prepare marinade up to 1 day in advance. Cover and refrigerate.

| | | |
|---|---|---|
| 2 | cloves garlic, minced | 2 |
| 1/2 cup | chopped fresh oregano (or 1 tbsp/15 mL dried) | 125 mL |
| 1/4 cup | chopped fresh parsley | 50 mL |
| 1/4 cup | freshly squeezed lemon juice | 50 mL |
| 1 tbsp | olive oil | 15 mL |
| 1/2 tsp | kosher salt | 2 mL |
| 1/4 tsp | freshly ground black pepper | 1 mL |
| 4 | boneless, skinless chicken breasts | 4 |

1. In a small bowl, whisk together garlic, oregano, parsley, lemon juice, olive oil, salt and pepper.

2. Place chicken breasts in a shallow dish. Brush marinade on chicken, coating evenly. Cover and refrigerate for a minimum of 20 minutes or for up to 1 day. Meanwhile, preheat contact grill.

3. Spray both sides of contact grill with vegetable cooking spray or oil. Place chicken on grill, close lid and grill for 5 to 6 minutes, or until chicken is no longer pink inside and reaches an internal temperature of 170°F (75°C).

**Variation**

This dish can easily be transformed into chicken souvlaki by slicing the chicken into 1-inch (2.5 cm) chunks and threading onto soaked 9-inch (23 cm) bamboo skewers before grilling. Grill for 5 to 6 minutes, or until chicken is no longer pink inside.

# Pesto Chicken Thighs

*Your family will love this fabulous gourmet grill, but it's also an impressive meal for guests.*

If your contact grill has more than one temperature setting, set it to high for this recipe.

**Tip**
This recipe requires a longer grilling time to ensure the coating is crispy.

| ⅓ cup | pesto, homemade (see recipe, opposite) or prepared | 75 mL |
| ½ cup | dry bread crumbs | 125 mL |
| 2 tbsp | freshly grated Parmesan cheese | 25 mL |
| ¼ tsp | salt | 1 mL |
| ¼ tsp | freshly ground black pepper | 1 mL |
| 8 | boneless, skinless chicken thighs | 8 |

1. Place pesto in a small bowl.
2. In a shallow bowl, mix together bread crumbs, Parmesan, salt and pepper.
3. Brush chicken thighs with pesto and roll in bread crumbs, coating evenly. Place in a shallow dish, cover and refrigerate for a minimum of 20 minutes or for up to 1 hour. Discard any excess pesto or crumbs. Meanwhile, preheat contact grill.
4. Spray both sides of contact grill with vegetable cooking spray or oil. Spray chicken thighs using a spray pump filled with olive oil or vegetable oil. Place chicken on grill, close lid and grill for 6 to 7 minutes, or until juices run clear when chicken is pierced, chicken reaches an internal temperature of 170°F (75°C) and coating is crispy.

**Variation**
Use 4 boneless, skinless chicken breasts in place of chicken thighs. Grill for same amount of time.

# Pesto

| 2 to 3 | cloves garlic | 2 to 3 |
| 1¼ cups | fresh basil leaves | 300 mL |
| ⅔ cup | pine nuts, toasted (see tip, at left) | 150 mL |
| ⅔ cup | olive oil | 150 mL |

**Tips**

Take advantage of abundant fresh basil in late August.

Pesto can be frozen for up to 2 months. If desired, freeze pesto in small, resealable freezer bags for easy access.

Toast pine nuts in a nonstick skillet over medium heat for about 2 minutes, turning occasionally until lightly browned.

In place of pine nuts, you can use toasted slivered almonds — but the flavor will not be as rich.

1. In a food processor, finely mince garlic. Add basil leaves and pine nuts and process until chopped. Pour in olive oil while processor is running. Process until smooth.

**Variation**

For the recipe above, or if you plan on freezing your pesto, do not use Parmesan cheese. But, if using as sauce over pasta, add ⅔ cup (150 mL) freshly grated Parmesan at the end, and process with a few on/off pulses just until combined.

# Grilled Chicken Cacciatore

*Hunter stew, also known as chicken cacciatore, is sublime when you use your indoor grill. The intensely flavored grilled vegetables and chicken take this comfort food to a gourmet level.*

If your contact grill has more than one temperature setting, set it to high for this recipe.

**Tip**

Sprinkle freshly grated Parmesan cheese on each individual serving.

**Make Ahead**

Grill vegetables and chicken up to 1 day in advance. Cover and refrigerate until ready to use, then add vegetables and chicken to pasta sauce. In a large saucepan, over medium heat, warm cacciatore until heated through.

| | | |
|---|---|---|
| 8 | boneless, skinless chicken thighs | 8 |
| 2 cups | cauliflower florets (about 8 oz/250g) | 500 mL |
| 2 cups | broccoli florets (about 8 oz/250g) | 500 mL |
| 1 | onion, quartered | 1 |
| 1/2 | green bell pepper, cut into 1-inch (2.5 cm) chunks | 1/2 |
| 1/2 | red bell pepper, cut into 1-inch (2.5 cm) chunks | 1/2 |
| 1 | zucchini, sliced in 1/4-inch (0.5 cm) rounds | 1 |
| 1 cup | mushrooms, halved | 250 mL |
| 12 oz | multigrain spaghetti | 375 g |
| 1 | can (22 oz/680 mL) zesty Italian pasta sauce | 1 |

**Chicken Rub**

| | | |
|---|---|---|
| 1 1/2 tsp | dried Italian seasoning | 7 mL |
| 1/2 tsp | garlic powder | 2 mL |
| 1/4 tsp | kosher salt | 1 mL |
| 1/4 tsp | freshly ground black pepper | 1 mL |

**Vegetable Marinade**

| | | |
|---|---|---|
| 2 | cloves garlic, minced | 2 |
| 3 tbsp | olive oil | 45 mL |
| 2 tbsp | white wine vinegar | 25 mL |
| 1/2 tsp | dried basil | 2 mL |
| 1/2 tsp | dried oregano | 2 mL |
| Pinch | kosher salt | Pinch |
| Pinch | freshly ground black pepper | Pinch |

1. *Prepare chicken rub:* In a small bowl, stir together Italian seasoning, garlic powder, salt and pepper.

2. Place chicken in a shallow dish. Sprinkle half of the rub on one side of chicken. Flip chicken and sprinkle remaining rub on other side. Cover and refrigerate for a minimum of 20 minutes or for up to 1 day.

3. *Prepare vegetable marinade:* Whisk together garlic, olive oil, vinegar, basil, oregano, salt and pepper.

4. Place cauliflower and broccoli in a shallow dish and sprinkle with 2 tbsp (25 mL) of marinade. Toss to coat.

5. Separate onion into layers. Place in another shallow dish and sprinkle with 2 tsp (10 mL) marinade. Toss to coat.

6. Place green and red peppers in third shallow dish and sprinkle with $2\frac{1}{2}$ tbsp (12 mL) marinade. Toss to coat.

7. Place zucchini and mushrooms in a fourth shallow dish and sprinkle with $1\frac{1}{2}$ tbsp (22 mL) marinade. Toss to coat.

8. Marinate all vegetables at room temperature for a minimum of 20 minutes or for up to 2 hours. Meanwhile, preheat contact grill.

9. Preheat oven to 325°F (160°C). Place cauliflower and broccoli on grill, close lid and grill for 10 minutes, until tender-crisp. Transfer to a 13- by 9-inch (3 L) baking pan and keep warm in oven.

10. Place onions on grill, close lid and grill for 4 to 6 minutes. Add to pan and keep warm.

11. Place peppers on grill, close lid and grill for 4 minutes. Add to pan and keep warm.

12. Place zucchini and mushrooms on grill, close lid and grill for 3 minutes. Add to pan and keep warm.

13. Meanwhile, in a large pot of boiling salted water, cook spaghetti for about 9 minutes, or until al dente. Drain and return to pot. Cover with lid to keep noodles warm until ready to serve.

14. Spray both sides of contact grill with vegetable cooking spray or oil. Place marinated chicken thighs on grill, close lid and grill for 5 to 6 minutes, or until juices run clear when chicken is pierced and reaches an internal temperature of 170°F (75°C).

15. In a microwave-safe container with a cover, microwave pasta sauce on High for 4 to 5 minutes, until heated through, stirring after 2 minutes.

16. *Assemble chicken cacciatore:* Once chicken is grilled, slice into chunks. Add to spaghetti, along with grilled vegetables and heated pasta sauce. Mix well.

# Four-Ingredient Chicken

*This quick dish is simple yet divine. On a busy night when your family is asking, "What's for dinner?" whip this recipe up — and accept the compliments.*

If your contact grill has more than one temperature setting, set it to high for this recipe.

**Tip**
Freshly grated Parmesan cheese is a must for this recipe.

| | | |
|---|---|---|
| 1/3 cup | freshly grated Parmesan cheese | 75 mL |
| 1/3 cup | corn flakes crumbs | 75 mL |
| 8 | boneless, skinless chicken thighs | 8 |
| 1/3 cup | zesty Italian salad dressing | 75 mL |

1. In a shallow bowl, combine Parmesan cheese and corn flakes crumbs.

2. Place chicken thighs in a shallow dish. Pour salad dressing over chicken, turning chicken several times to coat evenly. Roll chicken in crumbs, coating evenly and place on plate or baking sheet. Cover and refrigerate for at least 20 minutes or for up to 1 hour. Discard any excess dressing and crumbs. Meanwhile, preheat contact grill to high.

3. Spray both sides of contact grill with vegetable cooking spray or oil. Place chicken on grill, close lid and grill for 6 to 7 minutes, or until juices run clear when chicken is pierced, chicken reaches an internal temperature of 170°F (75°C) and coating is crispy.

**Variation**
Season crumbs with 1/4 tsp (1 mL) each garlic powder, salt and black pepper.

# Cayenne Raspberry Chicken

*This unique pairing of cayenne with raspberry provides an unforgettable taste.*

If your contact grill has more than one temperature setting, set it to high for this recipe.

**Tip**
Raspberry vinegar is a must for this recipe.

**Make Ahead**
Prepare marinade up to 1 day in advance. Cover and refrigerate.

| | | |
|---|---|---|
| 2 tbsp | seedless raspberry jam | 25 mL |
| 2 tbsp | raspberry vinegar | 25 mL |
| 1/2 tsp | cayenne pepper | 2 mL |
| 1/2 tsp | paprika | 2 mL |
| 1/2 tsp | dry mustard powder | 2 mL |
| 1/2 tsp | kosher salt | 2 mL |
| 1/4 tsp | garlic powder | 1 mL |
| 1/4 tsp | freshly ground black pepper | 1 mL |
| 4 | boneless, skinless chicken breasts | 4 |

1. In a microwave-safe dish, melt raspberry jam in microwave, uncovered, on High for about 20 seconds. Stir in raspberry vinegar, cayenne, paprika, mustard, salt, garlic powder and pepper.

2. Place chicken breasts in a shallow dish. Brush marinade on chicken, coating evenly. Cover and refrigerate for a minimum of 20 minutes or for up to 1 hour. Meanwhile, preheat contact grill.

3. Spray both sides of contact grill with vegetable cooking spray or oil. Place chicken on grill, close lid and grill for 5 to 6 minutes, or until chicken is no longer pink inside and reaches an internal temperature of 170°F (75°C).

**Variation**
In place of raspberry jam, purée 2 tbsp (25 mL) fresh raspberries, straining out seeds if desired. Add 1 tbsp (15 mL) granulated sugar to the marinade.

# Mango Chicken

SERVES 4

*Zesty mango chutney gives this sweet-and-sour dish a boost.*

If your contact grill has more than one temperature setting, set it to high for this recipe.

### Tip
The most popular mango chutney is Major Grey's, available at many supermarkets and specialty food stores. If there are large chunks of mango in the chutney, chop finely before measuring.

### Make Ahead
Prepare marinade up to 1 day in advance. Cover and refrigerate.

| | | |
|---|---|---|
| 2 | cloves garlic, minced | 2 |
| 1/3 cup | mango chutney (see tip, at left) | 75 mL |
| 1 tbsp | minced gingerroot | 15 mL |
| 1 tbsp | cider vinegar | 15 mL |
| 1 tbsp | soy sauce | 15 mL |
| 1/4 tsp | kosher salt | 1 mL |
| 1/4 tsp | freshly ground black pepper | 1 mL |
| 4 | boneless, skinless chicken breasts | 4 |

1. In a small bowl, whisk together garlic, chutney, gingerroot, vinegar, soy sauce, salt and pepper.
2. Place chicken breasts in a shallow dish. Brush marinade on chicken, coating evenly. Cover and refrigerate for a minimum of 20 minutes or for up to 1 hour. Meanwhile, preheat contact grill.
3. Spray both sides of contact grill with vegetable cooking spray or oil. Place chicken on grill, close lid and grill for 5 to 6 minutes, or until chicken is no longer pink inside and reaches an internal temperature of 170°F (75°C).

### Variation
Use 8 boneless, skinless chicken thighs in place of chicken breasts. Grill for same amount of time.

# Coconut Mango Chicken Breasts

*Fresh mango and grilled chicken breasts are a dynamic duo.*

If your contact grill has more than one temperature setting, set it to high for this recipe.

**Make Ahead**
Prepare marinade up to 1 day in advance. Cover and refrigerate.

| | | |
|---|---|---|
| 1 | clove garlic | 1 |
| 1 tsp | chopped gingerroot | 5 mL |
| 1/2 cup | chopped peeled fresh mango | 125 mL |
| 1/3 cup | coconut milk | 75 mL |
| 1/2 tsp | ground coriander | 2 mL |
| 1/2 tsp | curry powder | 2 mL |
| 1/4 tsp | kosher salt | 1 mL |
| 1/4 tsp | freshly ground black pepper | 1 mL |
| 4 | boneless, skinless chicken breasts | 4 |
| 1/4 cup | coconut (see tip, at left) | 50 mL |

1. In a food processor, finely mince garlic and gingerroot. Add mango and process with one or two on/off pulses. Add coconut milk, coriander, curry powder, salt and pepper. Process until smooth.

2. Place chicken breasts in a shallow dish. Brush marinade on chicken, coating evenly. Cover and refrigerate for a minimum of 20 minutes or for up to 1 hour. Meanwhile, preheat contact grill.

3. Spray both sides of contact grill with vegetable cooking spray or oil. Dip marinated chicken in toasted coconut. Discard any excess marinade and coconut. Place chicken on grill, close lid and grill for 6 minutes, or until chicken is no longer pink inside and reaches an internal temperature of 170°F (75°C).

**Variation**
Use 8 boneless, skinless chicken thighs in place of chicken breasts and add 1 to 2 tbsp (15 to 25 mL) more coconut. Grill for same amount of time.

# Cilantro Lime Chicken

*I prefer chicken thighs for this recipe because they remain juicy and capture the essence of the fresh herb and lime combination.*

If your contact grill has more than one temperature setting, set it to high for this recipe.

**Tip**

Cilantro, sometimes called Chinese parsley, is an aromatic herb.

**Make Ahead**

Prepare marinade up to 1 day in advance. Cover and refrigerate.

| 2 | cloves garlic, minced | 2 |
|---|---|---|
| ¼ cup | chopped fresh cilantro | 50 mL |
| 1 tsp | grated lime zest | 5 mL |
| 2 tbsp | freshly squeezed lime juice | 25 mL |
| 2 tsp | olive oil | 10 mL |
| ½ tsp | cumin seeds | 2 mL |
| ½ tsp | kosher salt | 2 mL |
| ¼ tsp | freshly ground black pepper | 1 mL |
| 8 | boneless, skinless chicken thighs | 8 |

1. In a small bowl, whisk together garlic, cilantro, lime zest, lime juice, olive oil, cumin, salt and pepper.
2. Place chicken breasts in a shallow dish. Brush marinade on chicken, coating evenly. Cover and refrigerate for a minimum of 20 minutes or for up to 1 hour. Meanwhile, preheat contact grill.
3. Spray both sides of contact grill with vegetable cooking spray or oil. Place chicken on grill, close lid and grill for 5 to 6 minutes, or until juices run clear when chicken is pierced and chicken reaches an internal temperature of 170°F (75°C).

**Variation**
Use 4 boneless, skinless chicken breasts in place of chicken thighs. Grill for same amount of time.

# Ginger, Soy and Lime Chicken

**SERVES 4**

*The aroma from this recipe is mouthwatering — just like the grilled chicken.*

If your contact grill has more than one temperature setting, set it to high for this recipe.

**Tip**

Dark brown sugar is richer and more intensely flavored than golden brown sugar. It's a great addition to this recipe.

**Make Ahead**

Prepare marinade up to 1 day in advance. Cover and refrigerate.

| 1 | clove garlic, minced | 1 |
| 2 tbsp | freshly squeezed lime juice | 25 mL |
| 2 tbsp | soy sauce | 25 mL |
| 1½ tsp | minced gingerroot | 7 mL |
| 1 tsp | packed dark brown sugar | 5 mL |
| 4 | boneless, skinless chicken breasts | 4 |

1. In a small bowl, whisk together garlic, lime juice, soy sauce, gingerroot and brown sugar.

2. Place chicken breasts between two pieces of wax paper. Pound until flattened to about ½ inch (1 cm) thick and place in a shallow dish. Brush marinade on chicken, coating evenly. Cover and refrigerate for a minimum of 20 minutes or for up to 1 hour. Meanwhile, preheat contact grill.

3. Spray both sides of contact grill with vegetable cooking spray or oil. Place chicken on grill, close lid and grill for 5 to 6 minutes, or until chicken is no longer pink inside and reaches an internal temperature of 170°F (75°C).

**Variation**

Use 8 boneless, skinless chicken thighs in place of chicken breasts. Grill for same amount of time.

# Orange Sesame Chicken

**SERVES 4**

*I love the combination of orange and sesame, especially when paired with chicken. Serve with couscous (see recipe, right).*

If your contact grill has more than one temperature setting, set it to high for this recipe.

**Tip**

Fresh gingerroot supplies a more intense flavor than ground ginger. Store gingerroot at room temperature in open air; it will keep for about 1 month.

**Make Ahead**

Prepare marinade up to 1 day in advance. Cover and refrigerate.

| | | |
|---|---|---|
| 1 | clove garlic, minced | 1 |
| 1/2 tsp | grated orange zest | 2 mL |
| 1/4 cup | freshly squeezed orange juice | 50 mL |
| 2 tbsp | liquid honey | 25 mL |
| 1 tbsp | soy sauce | 15 mL |
| 1 tsp | sesame oil | 5 mL |
| 1 tsp | minced gingerroot | 5 mL |
| 1/4 tsp | kosher salt | 1 mL |
| 1/4 tsp | freshly ground black pepper | 1 mL |
| 4 | boneless, skinless chicken breasts | 4 |

1. In a small bowl, whisk together garlic, orange zest, orange juice, honey, soy sauce, sesame oil, gingerroot, salt and pepper.

2. Place chicken breasts in a shallow dish. Brush marinade on chicken, coating evenly. Cover and refrigerate for a minimum of 20 minutes or for up to 1 hour. Meanwhile, preheat contact grill.

3. Spray both sides of contact grill with vegetable cooking spray or oil. Place chicken on grill, close lid and grill for 5 to 6 minutes, or until chicken is no longer pink inside and reaches an internal temperature of 170°F (75°C).

**Variations**

Use 8 boneless, skinless chicken thighs in place of chicken breasts. Grill for same amount of time.

Dip marinated chicken in 1 beaten egg and then in 2/3 cup (150 mL) panko crumbs (see tip, page 75) seasoned with 1/4 tsp (1 mL) each salt and pepper. Place chicken on grill, close lid and grill for 6 to 7 minutes, or until juices run clear when chicken is pierced, chicken reaches an internal temperature of 170°F (75°C) and coating is crispy.

# Couscous

**MAKES ABOUT
3 CUPS (750 ML)**

| | | |
|---|---|---|
| 1 cup | water | 250 mL |
| 1/4 cup | freshly squeezed orange juice | 50 mL |
| 1/2 tsp | ground cinnamon | 2 mL |
| 1/4 tsp | ground cloves | 1 mL |
| 1/4 tsp | ground ginger | 1 mL |
| 1/4 tsp | powdered turmeric | 1 mL |
| 1 cup | couscous | 250 mL |
| 1/2 cup | currants | 125 mL |

1. In a medium saucepan, bring water, orange juice, cinnamon, cloves, ginger and turmeric to a boil. Stir in couscous. Remove from heat.

2. Let stand for 5 minutes, covered, until liquid is absorbed. Fluff with a fork. Stir in currants.

**Variation**

In place of water and orange juice, use chicken broth. Replace cinnamon, cloves, ginger and turmeric with 1 tsp (5 mL) dried thyme leaves. Instead of currants, add 1/2 cup (125 mL) chopped green olives with pimientos. Season with freshly ground black pepper to taste.

# Szechuan Chicken

**SERVES 4**

*Anyone with a penchant
for the piquant will enjoy
this fiery dish.*

If your contact grill
has more than one
temperature setting,
set it to high for
this recipe.

| | | |
|---|---|---|
| 2 tsp | peanut oil | 10 mL |
| 2 | cloves garlic, minced | 2 |
| 1 | small dried chili pepper, minced | 1 |
| 1½ tsp | grated orange zest | 7 mL |
| 1½ tsp | minced gingerroot | 7 mL |
| ½ cup + 1 tbsp | freshly squeezed orange juice, divided | 140 mL |
| 2 tbsp | rice vinegar | 25 mL |
| 2 tbsp | soy sauce | 25 mL |
| 1 tsp | cornstarch | 5 mL |
| 4 | boneless, skinless chicken breasts | 4 |

1. In a small saucepan, heat oil over medium heat. Sauté garlic, chili pepper, orange zest and gingerroot for 3 minutes, until softened. Add ½ cup (125 mL) of the orange juice, vinegar and soy sauce. Bring to a boil.

2. Dissolve cornstarch in the remaining 1 tbsp (15 mL) orange juice. Stir into sauce. Reduce heat and simmer, stirring, for 5 minutes, until thickened and glossy. Let cool.

3. Place chicken breasts in a shallow dish. Brush marinade on chicken, coating evenly. Cover and refrigerate for a minimum of 20 minutes or for up to 1 hour. Meanwhile, preheat contact grill.

4. Spray both sides of contact grill with vegetable cooking spray or oil. Place chicken on grill, close lid and grill for 5 to 6 minutes, or until chicken is no longer pink inside and reaches an internal temperature of 170°F (75°C).

## Tips

If you don't have whole chili peppers on hand, use ½ to 1 tsp (2 to 5 mL) hot pepper flakes. If you want this dish to be even hotter, use a large dried chili pepper or more hot pepper flakes. Downgrade the heat factor by reducing the amount of chili pepper or hot pepper flakes.

If desired, before marinating the chicken, set aside ¼ cup (50 mL) of the sauce to drizzle on cooked chicken after it is grilled.

## Make Ahead

Prepare marinade up to 1 day in advance. Cover and refrigerate.

Maple-Glazed Pork Chops (page 159)

*Overleaf:* Caesar Burgers (page 71)

# Sticky Sesame Chicken

*Kids are drawn to this "sticky chicky" recipe, another quick weekday meal.*

If your contact grill has more than one temperature setting, set it to high for this recipe.

**Make Ahead**
Prepare marinade up to 1 day in advance. Cover and refrigerate.

| 2 | cloves garlic, minced | 2 |
|---|---|---|
| ¼ cup | oyster sauce | 50 mL |
| 1 tbsp | freshly squeezed lemon juice | 15 mL |
| 1 tbsp | liquid honey | 15 mL |
| 1 tsp | sesame oil | 5 mL |
| ¼ tsp | freshly ground black pepper | 1 mL |
| 4 | boneless, skinless chicken breasts | 4 |
| 2 tbsp | sesame seeds | 25 mL |

1. In a small bowl, whisk together garlic, oyster sauce, lemon juice, honey, sesame oil and pepper.

2. Place chicken breasts in a shallow dish. Brush marinade on chicken, coating evenly. Cover and refrigerate for a minimum of 20 minutes or for up to 1 hour. Meanwhile, preheat contact grill.

3. Spray both sides of contact grill with vegetable cooking spray or oil. Sprinkle sesame seeds on both sides of chicken. Place chicken on grill, close lid and grill for 5 to 6 minutes, or until chicken is no longer pink inside and reaches an internal temperature of 170°F (75°C).

### Variations
Use 8 boneless, skinless chicken thighs in place of chicken breasts. Grill for same amount of time.

Add 1 tsp (5 mL) minced gingerroot or ¼ tsp (1 mL) ground ginger to marinade.

Sausage and Vegetable Herbed Pasta Toss (page 164)

# Teriyaki Chicken

SERVES 4

*This dish with its homemade teriyaki sauce is simply delicious. You won't need to rely on frozen, prepackaged teriyaki chicken after trying this straightforward recipe. Serve with pasta and steamed broccoli.*

If your contact grill has more than one temperature setting, set it to high for this recipe.

**Make Ahead**

Marinate chicken overnight, or prepare before going to work and marinate all day.

| | | |
|---|---|---|
| 2 | cloves garlic, minced | 2 |
| 3 tbsp | soy sauce | 45 mL |
| 1 tbsp | minced gingerroot | 15 mL |
| 2 tsp | sherry | 10 mL |
| 1 tsp | granulated sugar | 5 mL |
| 4 | boneless, skinless chicken breasts | 4 |

1. In a small bowl, whisk together garlic, soy sauce, gingerroot, sherry and sugar.

2. Place chicken breasts in a shallow dish. Brush marinade on chicken, coating evenly. Cover and refrigerate for a minimum of 20 minutes. Meanwhile, preheat contact grill to high.

3. Spray both sides of contact grill with vegetable cooking spray or oil. Place chicken on grill, close lid and grill for 5 to 6 minutes, or until chicken is no longer pink inside and reaches an internal temperature of 170°F (75°C).

**Variation**

Dip marinated chicken in 1 beaten egg and then in $\frac{2}{3}$ cup (150 mL) panko crumbs (see tip, page 75) seasoned with $\frac{1}{4}$ tsp (1 mL) each salt and pepper before grilling. Place chicken on grill, close lid and grill for 6 to 7 minutes, or until juices run clear when chicken is pierced, chicken reaches an internal temperature of 170°F (75°C) and coating is crispy.

# Green Peppercorn and Gruyère Turkey Fillets

*Green peppercorns and strong Gruyère cheese marry well with boneless, skinless turkey breast.*

If your contact grill has more than one temperature setting, set it to high for this recipe.

**Tip**

Swiss Gruyère is a robust cheese that is excellent for melting.

**Make Ahead**

Prepare dry rub up to 1 day in advance. Cover and refrigerate.

| | | |
|---|---|---|
| 1 1/2 tsp | drained and crushed green peppercorns (see tip, page 102) | 7 mL |
| 1/2 tsp | salt | 2 mL |
| 1/2 tsp | garlic powder | 2 mL |
| 1/2 tsp | dried thyme | 2 mL |
| 1 | boneless, skinless turkey breast (about 1 lb/500 g) | 1 |
| 2 oz | Gruyère cheese, sliced thinly | 60 g |

1. In a small bowl, combine peppercorns, salt, garlic powder and thyme.

2. Slice turkey breast crosswise into 4 equal portions, then slice each piece horizontally about three-quarters of the way through to butterfly. Lay the butterflied turkey portions flat in a shallow dish and, using your fingers, coat with dry rub, coating evenly. Cover and refrigerate for a minimum of 20 minutes or for up to 1 day. Meanwhile, preheat contact grill.

3. Spray both sides of contact grill with vegetable cooking spray or oil. Place turkey on grill, close lid and grill for 6 minutes. After 6 minutes, place 1 or 2 thin slices of Gruyère on half of each turkey portion. Fold the other half over the cheese. Close lid and grill for another 1 to 2 minutes, or until cheese has melted and turkey is no longer pink inside and reaches an internal temperature of 170°F (75°C).

**Variation**

For a zesty dish, use spiced Gouda with cumin seeds in place of Gruyère.

# Orange Rosemary Turkey Thighs

*For a no-fuss turkey dinner, this is your ticket.*

If your contact grill has more than one temperature setting, set it to high for this recipe.

**Tip**
Meaty turkey thighs offer a different taste and texture than their chicken cousins.

**Make Ahead**
Prepare marinade up to 1 day in advance. Cover and refrigerate.

| | | |
|---|---|---|
| 2 | cloves garlic, minced | 2 |
| 1 | sprig fresh rosemary (or ³⁄₄ tsp/4 mL dried) | 1 |
| 1 tsp | grated orange zest | 5 mL |
| ¼ cup | freshly squeezed orange juice | 50 mL |
| 1 tbsp | Dijon mustard | 15 mL |
| ½ tsp | kosher salt | 2 mL |
| ¼ tsp | freshly ground black pepper | 1 mL |
| 2 | boneless, skinless turkey thighs (about 1 lb/500 g) | 2 |

1. In a small bowl, whisk together garlic, rosemary, orange zest, orange juice, mustard, salt and pepper.

2. Place turkey thighs between two pieces of wax paper. Pound until flattened to about ½ inch (1 cm) thick. Cut each turkey thigh in half and place in a shallow dish. Brush marinade on turkey, coating evenly. Cover and refrigerate for a minimum of 20 minutes or for up to 1 hour. Meanwhile, preheat contact grill.

3. Spray both sides of contact grill with vegetable cooking spray or oil. Place turkey on grill, close lid and grill for 6 to 7 minutes, or until juices run clear when turkey is pierced and turkey reaches an internal temperature of 170°F (75°C).

**Variation**
Use 8 boneless, skinless chicken thighs in place of turkey thighs. Grill for 6 minutes, or until chicken juices run clear when chicken is pierced and chicken reaches an internal temperature of 170°F (75°C).

# Main Entrées:
# Fish and Seafood

Blackened Red Fish . . . . . . . . . . . . . . . . . . . . . . . . . . . 134

"Fried" Catfish . . . . . . . . . . . . . . . . . . . . . . . . . . . . . . 136

Herbed Halibut . . . . . . . . . . . . . . . . . . . . . . . . . . . . . . 137

Lemon-Pepper Fish Fillets . . . . . . . . . . . . . . . . . . . . . . 138

"Pan-Fried" Grilled Pickerel . . . . . . . . . . . . . . . . . . . . 140

Mustard Lemon Herb Rainbow Trout . . . . . . . . . . . . 141

Sweet-and-Sour Rainbow Trout . . . . . . . . . . . . . . . . . 142

Cumin Lemon Tuna Steaks . . . . . . . . . . . . . . . . . . . . 143

Honey Dill Salmon with Dijon . . . . . . . . . . . . . . . . . 144

Honey Orange Salmon with Thyme . . . . . . . . . . . . . . 145

Lemon Honey Dill Salmon . . . . . . . . . . . . . . . . . . . . . 146

Orange Soy Ginger–Glazed Salmon . . . . . . . . . . . . . . 147

Oriental Salmon Steaks . . . . . . . . . . . . . . . . . . . . . . . 148

Salmon Patties . . . . . . . . . . . . . . . . . . . . . . . . . . . . . 149

Lemon Herb Shrimp . . . . . . . . . . . . . . . . . . . . . . . . . 150

Moroccan Shrimp . . . . . . . . . . . . . . . . . . . . . . . . . . . 151

Singapore Shrimp . . . . . . . . . . . . . . . . . . . . . . . . . . . 152

Susie's Lime Shrimp . . . . . . . . . . . . . . . . . . . . . . . . . 153

Thai Shrimp . . . . . . . . . . . . . . . . . . . . . . . . . . . . . . . 154

# Blackened Red Fish

*This taste of New Orleans delights all of the senses.*

If your contact grill has more than one temperature setting, set it to medium-high for this recipe.

## Tips

You can use store-bought Cajun seasoning in place of homemade Cajun Spice Blend.

Due to the acidic nature of lime juice, do not marinate snapper fillets for longer than 1 hour.

## Make Ahead

Cajun Spice Blend can be prepared in advance and stored in an airtight container in a cool, dry place for up to 2 months.

| | | |
|---|---|---|
| 3 tbsp | Cajun Spice Blend (see recipe opposite) | 45 mL |
| 1 1/2 tbsp | dried onion flakes | 22 mL |
| 1 lb | red snapper fillets, cut into 4 pieces | 500 g |
| | Juice of 1/2 lime | |

1. In a small bowl, stir together Cajun Spice Blend and onion flakes.

2. Dip snapper fillets in lime juice and then coat in Cajun dry rub. Place in a shallow dish, cover and refrigerate for a minimum of 20 minutes or for up to 1 hour. Meanwhile, preheat contact grill.

3. Spray both sides of contact grill with vegetable cooking spray or oil. Place fish fillets on grill, close lid and grill for 4 to 6 minutes, or until fish is opaque and flakes easily with a fork and coating is blackened.

### Variation
Use other firm-fleshed fish, such as catfish, in place of snapper. Grill for 4 to 6 minutes, or until fish is opaque and flakes easily with a fork.

# Cajun Spice Blend

**YIELD: 3 TBSP**

**Tips**

Recipe may be doubled or tripled.

Feel free to adjust Cajun Spice Blend to suit your own tastes. But ensure that your herbs and spices are fresh!

| | | |
|---|---|---|
| 1 tbsp | paprika | 15 mL |
| 1 tsp | cayenne pepper | 5 mL |
| 1 tsp | dried thyme | 5 mL |
| 1 tsp | garlic powder | 5 mL |
| 1 tsp | onion powder | 5 mL |
| 1/2 tsp | freshly ground white pepper | 2 mL |
| 1/2 tsp | freshly ground black pepper | 2 mL |
| 1/2 tsp | dried oregano | 2 mL |
| 1/2 tsp | kosher salt | 2 mL |

**1.** In a small bowl, combine paprika, cayenne pepper, thyme, garlic powder, onion powder, white pepper, black pepper, oregano and salt. Stir well.

# "Fried" Catfish

*Farmed catfish from the southern U.S. is readily available throughout the U.S. and Canada. If you can't find it, red snapper will work just fine.*

If your contact grill has more than one temperature setting, set it to medium-high for this recipe.

## Tip

You can use store-bought Cajun seasoning in place of homemade Cajun Spice Blend.

## Make Ahead

Cajun Spice Blend can be prepared in advance and stored in an airtight container in a cool, dry place for up to 3 months.

| | | |
|---|---|---|
| ⅓ cup | cornmeal | 75 mL |
| 2 tbsp | Cajun Spice Blend (see recipe, page 135) | 25 mL |
| 1 | egg | 1 |
| 1 lb | catfish or red snapper fillets, cut into 4 pieces | 500 g |

1. In a shallow dish, stir together cornmeal and Cajun Spice Blend. In a separate shallow dish, lightly beat egg to loosen.

2. Dip catfish fillets in beaten egg and then coat in cornmeal coating. Discard any excess egg and cornmeal mixture. Place fish in a shallow dish, cover and refrigerate for a minimum of 20 minutes or for up to 1 hour. Meanwhile, preheat contact grill.

3. Spray both sides of contact grill with vegetable cooking spray or oil. Place fish fillets on grill, close lid and grill for 5 to 6 minutes, or until fish is opaque and flakes easily with a fork and coating is crispy.

# Herbed Halibut

*Halibut steaks are a meaty fish that meld well with this herb marinade.*

If your contact grill has more than one temperature setting, set it to medium-high for this recipe.

**Make Ahead**

Prepare marinade up to 1 day in advance. Cover and refrigerate.

| | | |
|---|---|---|
| 2 | cloves garlic, minced | 2 |
| 2 tbsp | chopped fresh basil (or 2 tsp/10 mL dried) | 25 mL |
| 2 tbsp | freshly squeezed lemon juice | 25 mL |
| 1 tbsp | chopped fresh oregano (or 1 tsp/5 mL dried) | 15 mL |
| 1 tbsp | white wine vinegar | 15 mL |
| ½ tsp | salt | 2 mL |
| ¼ tsp | freshly ground black pepper | 1 mL |
| 4 | halibut steaks (each about 4 oz/125 g) | 4 |
| | Additional freshly squeezed lemon juice | |

1. In a small bowl, whisk together garlic, basil, lemon juice, oregano, vinegar, salt and pepper.

2. Place halibut steaks in a shallow dish and brush with marinade, coating evenly. Cover and refrigerate for a minimum of 20 minutes or for up to 1 hour. Meanwhile, preheat contact grill.

3. Spray both sides of contact grill with vegetable cooking spray or oil. Place halibut on grill, close lid and grill for 5 to 6 minutes, or until fish is opaque and flakes easily with a fork. Sprinkle with freshly squeezed lemon juice.

**Variations**

Use other firm steaks, such as tuna steaks, in place of halibut and grill for 5 to 6 minutes, or until fish is opaque and flakes easily with a fork.

Add other favorite herbs, such as ½ tsp (2 mL) dried thyme and 1 tbsp (15 mL) chopped fresh parsley, to the marinade.

# Lemon-Pepper Fish Fillets

**SERVES 4**

*Here's an easy way to increase your consumption of lower-fat, healthful fish. Serve with Tartar Sauce or Gremolata (see recipes, opposite).*

If your contact grill has more than one temperature setting, set it to medium-high for this recipe.

## Tip
If you don't have lemon pepper, use freshly ground black pepper and add 1 tsp (5 mL) grated lemon zest to marinade.

## Make Ahead
Prepare marinade up to 1 day in advance. Cover and refrigerate.

| | | |
|---|---|---|
| 1 lb | walleye fillets, cut into 4 pieces | 500 g |
| ½ tsp | ground lemon pepper | 2 mL |
| ½ tsp | salt | 2 mL |
| 2 tbsp | freshly squeezed lemon juice | 25 mL |
| 1 tbsp | olive oil | 15 mL |
| 1 tsp | Dijon mayonnaise | 5 mL |
| 2 | cloves garlic, minced | 2 |
| ½ cup | finely minced onion | 125 mL |
| ½ cup | chopped fresh parsley | 125 mL |

1. Place fish fillets in a shallow dish and season both sides with lemon pepper and salt.

2. In a small bowl, whisk together lemon juice, olive oil and Dijon mayonnaise. Stir in garlic, onion and parsley. Brush marinade on fish fillets, coating evenly. Cover and refrigerate for a minimum of 20 minutes or for up to 1 hour. Meanwhile, preheat contact grill.

3. Spray both sides of contact grill with vegetable cooking spray or oil. Place walleye on grill, close lid and grill for 4 to 6 minutes, or until fish is opaque and flakes easily with a fork.

**Variation**
Use other firm white fillets, such as sole, whitefish or halibut in place of walleye.

# Tartar Sauce

**MAKES**
**⅓ CUP (75 ML)**

| | | |
|---|---|---|
| ¼ cup | mayonnaise | 50 mL |
| 2 tbsp | prepared relish | 25 mL |
| 2 tsp | hot salsa | 10 mL |
| 1 tsp | freshly squeezed lemon juice | 5 mL |

1. In a small bowl, stir together mayonnaise, relish, salsa and lemon juice. Mix well. Cover and refrigerate for a minimum of 20 minutes to allow flavors to blend or for up to 2 days.

# Gremolata

**MAKES**
**½ CUP (125 ML)**

| | | |
|---|---|---|
| 2 | cloves garlic, minced | 2 |
| ½ cup | chopped fresh parsley | 125 mL |
| 1 tbsp | fresh lemon zest, minced | 15 mL |

1. In a small bowl, mix together garlic, parsley and lemon zest.

**Tip**
Tastes great served as a garnish with Italian Veal Burgers (see recipe, page 78).

# "Pan-Fried" Grilled Walleye

*Savor the taste of "fried fish," minus the fat. Once you try it, this good-for-you fish dish will replace the traditional high-fat, pan-fried preparation method. Serve with Tartar Sauce (see recipe, page 139).*

If your contact grill has more than one temperature setting, set it to medium-high for this recipe.

### Tip
Breaded or coated fish takes 1 or 2 minutes longer on the grill.

### Make Ahead
Prepare coating up to 1 day in advance. Cover and refrigerate.

| | | |
|---|---|---|
| ⅓ cup | cornmeal | 75 mL |
| ⅓ cup | whole wheat flour | 75 mL |
| 1 tsp | freshly ground black pepper | 5 mL |
| ½ tsp | garlic powder | 2 mL |
| ½ tsp | salt | 2 mL |
| 1 lb | walleye fillets, cut into 4 pieces | 500 g |
| 1 | egg | 1 |

1. In a shallow dish, combine cornmeal, flour, pepper, garlic powder and salt. In a separate shallow dish, lightly beat egg to loosen.

2. Dip pickerel fillets in egg and then in coating. Place in a shallow dish, cover and refrigerate for 15 minutes to allow coating to set. Discard any excess egg and cornmeal mixture. Meanwhile, preheat contact grill.

3. Spray both sides of contact grill with vegetable cooking spray or oil. Place walleye on grill, close lid and grill for 5 to 6 minutes, or until fish is opaque and flakes easily with a fork and coating is crispy.

### Variation
Spice up the coating by adding ½ tsp (2 mL) red pepper flakes and a pinch of cayenne pepper.

# Mustard Lemon Herb Rainbow Trout

*The addition of Dijon mustard to the herbes de Provence–spiked marinade brings French flair to the rainbow trout.*

If your contact grill has more than one temperature setting, set it to medium-high for this recipe and grill for 4 to 5 minutes.

**Make Ahead**

Prepare marinade up to 1 day in advance. Cover and refrigerate.

| | | |
|---|---|---:|
| 1 | clove garlic, minced | 1 |
| 1 tsp | grated lemon zest | 5 mL |
| 2 tbsp | freshly squeezed lemon juice | 25 mL |
| 1 tbsp | Dijon mustard | 15 mL |
| 1/2 tsp | *herbes de Provence* (see tip, page 72) | 2 mL |
| 1/2 tsp | salt | 2 mL |
| 1/4 tsp | freshly ground black pepper | 1 mL |
| 1 lb | rainbow trout fillets, cut into 4 pieces | 500 g |
| | Additional freshly squeezed lemon juice | |

1. In a small bowl, whisk together garlic, lemon zest, lemon juice, mustard, *herbes de Provence*, salt and pepper.

2. Place trout fillets in a shallow dish and brush with marinade, coating evenly. Cover and refrigerate for a minimum of 20 minutes or for up to 1 hour. Meanwhile, preheat contact grill.

3. Spray both sides of contact grill with vegetable cooking spray or oil. Place trout on grill, close lid and grill for 4 to 6 minutes, or until fish is opaque and flakes easily with a fork . Sprinkle with freshly squeezed lemon juice.

**Variations**

Use other firm fillets, such as steelhead trout, in place of rainbow trout. Grill for 5 to 6 minutes, or until fish is opaque and flakes easily with a fork.

Use an equal amount of grainy mustard in place of Dijon mustard for a more pronounced mustard flavor.

# Sweet-and-Sour Rainbow Trout

*Sweet apricot jam paired with sour cider vinegar produces an intense sweet-and-sour marinade that makes this rainbow trout sing.*

If your contact grill has more than one temperature setting, set it to medium-high for this recipe.

**Make Ahead**

Prepare marinade up to 1 day in advance. Cover and refrigerate.

| | | |
|---|---|---|
| ¼ cup | apricot jam | 50 mL |
| 1 | clove garlic, minced | 1 |
| 3 tbsp | cider vinegar | 45 mL |
| 1½ tbsp | dried onion flakes | 22 mL |
| ½ tsp | paprika | 2 mL |
| ½ tsp | salt | 2 mL |
| ¼ tsp | freshly ground black pepper | 1 mL |
| 1 lb | rainbow trout fillets, cut into 4 pieces | 500 g |

1. Spoon apricot jam into a small microwave-safe bowl or measuring cup. Microwave, uncovered, on High for about 20 seconds, or until melted. Whisk in garlic, vinegar, onion flakes, paprika, salt and pepper.

2. Place rainbow trout in a shallow dish and brush with marinade, coating evenly. Cover and refrigerate for a minimum of 20 minutes or for up to 1 hour. Meanwhile, preheat contact grill.

3. Spray both sides of contact grill with vegetable cooking spray or oil. Place trout on grill, close lid and grill for 4 to 6 minutes, or until fish is opaque and flakes easily with a fork.

**Variations**

Use apple jelly in place of apricot jam.
Use other firm fillets, such as steelhead trout, in place of rainbow trout. Grill for 5 to 6 minutes, or until fish is opaque and flakes easily with a fork.

# Cumin Lemon Tuna Steaks

*Tuna steaks sparkle when spiked with cumin seeds and fresh lemon juice.*

If your contact grill has more than one temperature setting, set it to medium-high for this recipe.

## Make Ahead
Prepare marinade up to 1 day in advance. Cover and refrigerate.

| 2 | cloves garlic, minced | 2 |
|---|---|---|
| 2 tsp | grated lemon zest | 10 mL |
| 2 tbsp | freshly squeezed lemon juice | 25 mL |
| 1 tsp | cumin seeds | 5 mL |
| 1 tsp | olive oil | 5 mL |
| 1/2 tsp | salt | 2 mL |
| 1/4 tsp | freshly ground black pepper | 1 mL |
| 4 | tuna steaks (each about 4 oz/125 g) | 4 |
| | Additional freshly squeezed lemon juice | |

1. In a small bowl, whisk together garlic, lemon zest, lemon juice, cumin seeds, olive oil, salt and pepper.

2. Place tuna steaks in a shallow dish and brush with marinade, coating evenly. Cover and refrigerate for a minimum of 20 minutes or for up to 1 hour. Meanwhile, preheat contact grill.

3. Spray both sides of contact grill with vegetable cooking spray or oil. Place tuna steaks on grill, close lid and grill for 5 to 6 minutes for medium, or until fish is opaque and flakes easily with a fork. Sprinkle with freshly squeezed lemon juice.

## Variations
Use other meaty fish, such as halibut steaks, in place of tuna and grill for 5 to 6 minutes for medium, or until fish is opaque and flakes easily with a fork.

For an even spicier marinade, add 1/4 teaspoon (1 mL) hot pepper flakes.

# Honey Dill Salmon with Dijon

*I wonder whether the indoor grill was created with salmon fillets in mind — they turn out that scrumptious.*

If your contact grill has more than one temperature setting, set it to medium-high for this recipe.

**Make Ahead**

Prepare marinade up to 1 day in advance. Cover and refrigerate.

| | | |
|---|---|---|
| 2 tbsp | chopped fresh dill | 25 mL |
| 2 tbsp | mayonnaise | 25 mL |
| 2 tbsp | Dijon mustard | 25 mL |
| 1 tbsp | liquid honey | 15 mL |
| 1/2 tsp | salt | 2 mL |
| 1/4 tsp | freshly ground black pepper | 1 mL |
| 1 lb | salmon fillet, cut into 4 pieces | 500 g |
| | Additional freshly squeezed lemon juice | |

1. In a small bowl, whisk together dill, mayonnaise, mustard, honey, salt and pepper.
2. Place salmon fillets in a shallow dish and brush with marinade, coating evenly. Cover and refrigerate for a minimum of 20 minutes or for up to 1 hour. Meanwhile, preheat contact grill.
3. Spray both sides of contact grill with vegetable cooking spray or oil. Place salmon on grill, close lid and grill for 4 to 6 minutes, or until fish is opaque and flakes easily with a fork. Sprinkle with freshly squeezed lemon juice.

**Variations**

Use other firm fillets, such as steelhead trout, in place of salmon and grill for 4 to 6 minutes, or until fish is opaque and flakes easily with a fork.

Use 2 tsp (10 mL) dried dillweed in place of fresh dill.

# Honey Orange Salmon with Thyme

SERVES 4

*There's no "thyme" like the present to incorporate more heart-healthy foods such as this flavor-packed fish into your diet.*

If your contact grill has more than one temperature setting, set it to medium-high for this recipe.

**Make Ahead**

Prepare marinade up to 1 day in advance. Cover and refrigerate.

| 2 | cloves garlic, minced | 2 |
| 1 tbsp | grated orange zest | 15 mL |
| 2 tbsp | freshly squeezed orange juice | 25 mL |
| 1 1/2 tbsp | chopped fresh thyme (or 1 1/2 tsp/7 mL dried) | 22 mL |
| 1 1/2 tbsp | chopped fresh parsley (or 1 1/2 tsp/7 mL dried) | 22 mL |
| 2 tsp | freshly squeezed lemon juice | 10 mL |
| 2 tsp | liquid honey | 10 mL |
| 1/2 tsp | salt | 2 mL |
| 1/4 tsp | freshly ground black pepper | 1 mL |
| 1 lb | salmon fillet, cut into 4 pieces | 500 g |
| | Additional freshly squeezed lemon juice | |

1. In a small bowl, whisk together garlic, orange zest, orange juice, thyme, parsley, lemon juice, honey, salt and pepper.

2. Place salmon fillets in a shallow dish and brush with marinade, coating evenly. Cover and refrigerate for a minimum of 20 minutes or for up to 1 hour. Meanwhile, preheat contact grill.

3. Spray both sides of contact grill with vegetable cooking spray or oil. Place salmon on grill, close lid and grill for 4 to 6 minutes, or until fish is opaque and flakes easily with a fork. Sprinkle with freshly squeezed lemon juice.

**Variation**

Use other firm fillets, such as steelhead trout, in place of salmon and cook for 4 to 6 minutes, or until fish is opaque and flakes easily with a fork.

# Lemon Honey Dill Salmon

*The combination of fresh lemon juice, sweet honey and flavorful dill can't be beaten.*

If your contact grill has more than one temperature setting, set it to medium-high for this recipe.

**Make Ahead**

Prepare marinade up to 1 day in advance. Cover and refrigerate.

| | | |
|---|---|---|
| 1 | clove garlic, minced | 1 |
| 2 tbsp | chopped fresh dill | 25 mL |
| ½ tsp | grated lemon zest | 2 mL |
| 2 tbsp | freshly squeezed lemon juice | 25 mL |
| 2 tbsp | liquid honey | 25 mL |
| ¼ tsp | salt | 1 mL |
| ¼ tsp | freshly ground black pepper | 1 mL |
| 1 lb | salmon fillet, cut into 4 pieces | 500 g |
| | Additional freshly squeezed lemon juice | |

1. In a small bowl, whisk together garlic, dill, lemon zest, lemon juice, honey, salt and pepper.
2. Place salmon fillets in a shallow dish and brush with marinade, coating evenly. Cover and refrigerate for a minimum of 20 minutes or for up to 1 hour. Meanwhile, preheat contact grill.
3. Spray both sides of contact grill with vegetable cooking spray or oil. Place salmon on grill, close lid and grill for 4 to 6 minutes, or until fish is opaque and flakes easily with a fork. Sprinkle with freshly squeezed lemon juice.

**Variations**

Use other firm fillets, such as steelhead trout, in place of salmon and grill for 4 to 6 minutes, or until fish is opaque and flakes easily with a fork.

Use an equal amount of grated orange zest and freshly squeezed orange juice in place of lemon zest and juice.

# Orange Soy Ginger–Glazed Salmon

SERVES 4

*This Asian-influenced salmon fillet, coated in toasted sesame seeds, teams well with brown rice and stir-fried vegetables.*

If your contact grill has more than one temperature setting, set it to medium-high for this recipe.

**Tip**
Toast sesame seeds in small nonstick skillet, over medium heat, for 3 to 5 minutes, or until golden brown.

**Make Ahead**
Prepare marinade up to 1 day in advance. Cover and refrigerate.

| | | |
|---|---|---|
| 2 | cloves garlic, minced | 2 |
| 1 tsp | grated orange zest | 5 mL |
| ¼ cup | freshly squeezed orange juice | 50 mL |
| 3 tbsp | soy sauce | 45 mL |
| 1½ tsp | minced gingerroot | 7 mL |
| 1 lb | salmon fillet, cut into 4 pieces | 500 g |
| 2 tbsp | toasted sesame seeds (see tip, at left) | 25 mL |
| | Additional freshly squeezed lemon juice | |

1. In a small bowl, whisk together garlic, orange zest, orange juice, soy sauce and gingerroot.

2. Place salmon fillets in a shallow dish and brush with marinade, coating evenly. Cover and refrigerate for a minimum of 20 minutes or for up to 1 hour. Meanwhile, preheat contact grill.

3. Spray both sides of contact grill with vegetable cooking spray or oil. Sprinkle toasted sesame seeds on salmon fillets. Place salmon on grill, close lid and grill for 4 to 6 minutes, or until fish is opaque and flakes easily with a fork. Sprinkle with freshly squeezed lemon juice.

**Variation**
Use other firm fillets, such as steelhead trout, in place of salmon and cook for 4 to 6 minutes, or until fish is opaque and flakes easily with a fork.

# Oriental Salmon Steaks

| | | |
|---|---|---|
| ¾ cup | soy sauce | 175 mL |
| 1 tbsp | olive oil | 15 mL |
| 1 tsp | hot pepper sauce | 5 mL |
| ½ tsp | garlic powder | 2 mL |
| ¼ tsp | freshly ground black pepper | 1 mL |
| | Juice of 1 lime | |
| 4 | large salmon steaks (about ¾ inch/2 cm thick) | 4 |

*Salmon steaks are great on the grill — they're even tasty the next day served at room temperature with fresh lemon wedges.*

1. In a small bowl, whisk together soy sauce, ¾ cup (175 mL) water, olive oil, hot pepper sauce, garlic powder, pepper and lime juice.

2. Place salmon steaks in a shallow dish. Pour marinade over salmon, turning several times to coat evenly. Cover and refrigerate for a minimum of 2 hours. Meanwhile, preheat contact grill.

3. Spray both sides of contact grill with vegetable cooking spray or oil. Place salmon on grill, close lid and grill for 5 to 6 minutes, or until fish is opaque and flakes easily with a fork. Discard any excess marinade.

If your contact grill has more than one temperature setting, set it to medium-high for this recipe.

### Variation

Use tuna or halibut steaks in place of salmon steaks and grill for 5 to 6 minutes, or until fish is opaque and flakes easily with a fork.

## Tip

Salmon steaks tend to be a little "fishier" tasting than salmon fillets and therefore benefit from marinating overnight.

## Make Ahead

Prepare marinade and marinate salmon up to 1 day in advance. Cover and refrigerate until ready to grill. If desired, you can prepare the entire recipe, store it overnight in the refrigerator and serve the next day. Bring salmon to room temperature for 20 minutes before serving.

# Salmon Patties

*Salmon patties can be prepared with the more economical pink salmon rather than sockeye salmon and, thanks to the indoor grill, can be enjoyed as a lower-fat option compared to the traditional fried salmon patties.*

If your contact grill has more than one temperature setting, set it to high for this recipe.

**Tip**
If desired, serve as salmon burgers on Kaiser buns spread with Dijon mustard and mayonnaise and topped with lettuce, tomato and pickles.

**Make Ahead**
Prepare and grill salmon patties up to 1 day in advance. Cover and refrigerate. Heat on a baking sheet in a 350°F (180°C) oven for 20 minutes just before serving.

| | | |
|---|---|---|
| 1 tsp | olive oil | 5 mL |
| 1 | small onion, minced | 1 |
| 1 | clove garlic, minced | 1 |
| 2 | cans (each 7 oz/200 g) pink salmon, drained | 2 |
| ½ cup | dry bread crumbs | 125 mL |
| ¼ cup | chopped fresh parsley | 50 mL |
| ½ tsp | freshly ground black pepper | 2 mL |
| ¼ tsp | salt | 1 mL |

1. In a nonstick skillet, heat olive oil over medium-low heat. Sauté onion and garlic for about 5 minutes, until onions start to brown.

2. In a medium bowl, combine salmon, bread crumbs, parsley, pepper and salt. Stir in sautéed onion and garlic. Mix well. Form into 6 salmon patties, each about 3 inches (7.5 cm) in diameter. Cover and refrigerate for 20 minutes. Meanwhile, preheat contact grill.

3. Spray both sides of contact grill with vegetable cooking spray or oil. Spray both sides of salmon patties using a spray pump filled with olive oil or vegetable oil. Place patties on grill, close lid and grill for 7 to 8 minutes, or until patties are crisp on the outside and hot in the center.

**Variation**
Use an equal amount of canned tuna in place of pink salmon.

# Lemon Herb Shrimp

*This fast and easy dish is perfect for a busy weeknight.*

If your contact grill has more than one temperature setting, set it to medium-high for this recipe.

**Make Ahead**
Prepare marinade up to 1 day in advance. Cover and refrigerate.

• **Five to six 9-inch (23 cm) bamboo skewers**

| | | |
|---|---|---|
| 2 | cloves garlic, minced | 2 |
| 2 tbsp | freshly squeezed lemon juice | 25 mL |
| 1 tsp | dried marjoram | 5 mL |
| 1 tsp | dried oregano | 5 mL |
| 1 tsp | dried basil | 5 mL |
| 1/2 tsp | salt | 2 mL |
| 1/4 tsp | hot pepper flakes | 1 mL |
| 1/4 tsp | freshly ground black pepper | 2mL |
| 1 lb | large shrimp | 500 g |

1. Soak bamboo skewers in hot water for 30 minutes.

2. In a small bowl, whisk together garlic, lemon juice, marjoram, oregano, basil, salt, hot pepper flakes and pepper.

3. Shell and devein shrimp, keeping tail intact. Thread shrimp onto skewers. Place in a shallow dish and pour marinade over shrimp. Cover and refrigerate for a minimum of 20 minutes or for up to 1 hour. Meanwhile, preheat contact grill.

4. Spray both sides of contact grill with vegetable cooking spray or oil. Place shrimp skewers on grill, close lid and grill for 2 minutes, or until shrimp are pink and opaque.

**Variation**
Use 4 boneless, skinless chicken breasts or 8 chicken thighs cut into 1-inch (2.5 cm) cubes in place of shrimp. Thread onto skewers, marinate as directed and grill on high for 5 to 6 minutes, or until chicken is no longer pink inside and reaches an internal temperature of 170°F (75°C).

# Moroccan Shrimp

*Serve this dish with couscous (see recipe, page 127) rather than rice for a Moroccan-themed dinner.*

If your contact grill has more than one temperature setting, set it to medium-high for this recipe.

**Make Ahead**

Prepare marinade up to 1 day in advance. Cover and refrigerate.

| | | |
|---|---|---|
| 1 tsp | grated lemon zest | 5 mL |
| 3 tbsp | freshly squeezed lemon juice | 45 mL |
| 1 tsp | garlic powder | 5 mL |
| 1 tsp | dried parsley flakes (or 1 tbsp/15 mL chopped fresh parsley) | 5 mL |
| 1 tsp | ground coriander (or 1 tbsp/15 mL chopped fresh cilantro) | 5 mL |
| 1/2 tsp | paprika | 2 mL |
| 1/2 tsp | ground cumin | 2 mL |
| 1/4 tsp | salt | 1 mL |
| Pinch | freshly ground black pepper | Pinch |
| 1 lb | large shrimp | 500 g |

1. In a small bowl, whisk together lemon zest, lemon juice, garlic powder, parsley, coriander, paprika, cumin, salt and pepper.

2. Shell and devein shrimp, keeping tail intact. Place in a shallow dish and brush paste over shrimp, coating evenly. Cover and refrigerate for a minimum of 20 minutes or for up to 1 hour. Meanwhile, preheat contact grill.

3. Spray both sides of contact grill with vegetable cooking spray or oil. Place shrimp on grill, close lid and grill for 2 minutes, or until shrimp are pink and opaque.

**Variation**

Use 4 boneless, skinless chicken breasts or 8 chicken thighs in place of shrimp. Grill on high for 5 to 6 minutes, or until chicken is no longer pink inside and reaches an internal temperature of 170°F (75°C).

# Singapore Shrimp

*This zesty dish will spice up your life. Serve over Basmati rice for an enchanting entrée.*

If your contact grill has more than one temperature setting, set it to medium-high for this recipe.

**Make Ahead**

Prepare marinade up to 1 day in advance. Cover and refrigerate.

| | | |
|---|---|---|
| 1 tbsp | olive oil | 15 mL |
| 2 | cloves garlic, minced | 2 |
| 2 | green onions, minced | 2 |
| 1½ tbsp | minced gingerroot | 22 mL |
| ½ tsp | hot pepper flakes | 2 mL |
| 2½ tbsp | soy sauce | 32 mL |
| 1½ tbsp | oyster sauce | 22 mL |
| 1 tsp | packed brown sugar | 5 mL |
| ½ tsp | freshly ground black pepper | 2 mL |
| 1 lb | large shrimp | 500 g |

1. In a small saucepan, heat olive oil over medium heat. Sauté garlic, green onions and gingerroot for 2 minutes. Stir in hot pepper flakes. Add soy sauce, oyster sauce, brown sugar and pepper. Bring to a boil, stirring frequently. Reduce heat and simmer for 5 minutes, until sugar has dissolved and sauce has thickened. Let cool to room temperature.

2. Shell and devein shrimp, keeping tail intact. Place in a shallow dish and pour marinade over shrimp. Cover and refrigerate for a minimum of 20 minutes or for up to 1 hour. Meanwhile, preheat contact grill.

3. Spray both sides of contact grill with vegetable cooking spray or oil. Place shrimp on grill, close lid and grill for 2 minutes, or until shrimp are pink and opaque.

**Variation**
Use 4 boneless, skinless chicken breasts or 8 chicken thighs in place of shrimp. Grill on high for 5 to 6 minutes, or until chicken is no longer pink inside and reaches an internal temperature of 170°F (75°C).

# Susie's Lime Shrimp

*My friend Susie Strachan shared this sensational recipe for unique lime shrimp. It's not only delicious, but easy to prepare too!*

If your contact grill has more than one temperature setting, set it to medium-high for this recipe.

**Tip**
Use a milder salsa if desired.

**Make Ahead**
Grill shrimp up to 1 day in advance, cover and refrigerate. Serve chilled, à la shrimp cocktail.

| | | |
|---|---|---|
| 1 lb | jumbo shrimp | 500 g |
| 1 cup | hot salsa | 250 mL |
| 2 tbsp | thawed frozen limeade concentrate | 25 mL |

1. Shell and devein shrimp, keeping tail intact. Place shrimp in a shallow dish and pour salsa over shrimp, turning shrimp several times to coat evenly. Cover and refrigerate for a minimum of 20 minutes or for up to 1 hour. Meanwhile, preheat contact grill.

2. Spray both sides of contact grill with vegetable cooking spray or oil. Place shrimp on grill, close lid and grill for 2 minutes, or until shrimp are pink and opaque. Discard any excess salsa.

3. Place shrimp on a serving platter and drizzle with limeade concentrate. Serve immediately.

# Thai Shrimp

*Thai food is so popular today that it's become de rigueur at cafés and bistros. Why not tempt your family with Thai cuisine prepared in your own kitchen?*

If your contact grill has more than one temperature setting, set it to medium-high for this recipe.

## Tips

Coconut milk comes canned and can be found in Asian markets and most supermarkets.

Due to the acidic nature of lime juice, do not marinate shrimp for longer than 1 hour.

## Make Ahead

Prepare marinade up to 1 day in advance. Cover and refrigerate.

| | | |
|---|---|---|
| ¼ cup | coconut milk | 50 mL |
| 2 tsp | freshly squeezed lime juice | 10 mL |
| 2 tsp | chopped fresh basil | 10 mL |
| 1 tsp | chopped fresh cilantro | 5 mL |
| ½ tsp | chili garlic sauce | 2 mL |
| Pinch | kosher salt | Pinch |
| 1 lb | large shrimp | 500 g |

1. In a small bowl, whisk together coconut milk, lime juice, basil, cilantro, garlic sauce and salt.

2. Shell and devein shrimp, keeping tail intact. Place in a shallow dish and pour marinade over shrimp. Cover and refrigerate for a minimum of 20 minutes or for up to 1 hour. Meanwhile, preheat contact grill.

3. Spray both sides of contact grill with vegetable cooking spray or oil. Place shrimp on grill, close lid and grill for 2 minutes, or until shrimp are pink and opaque. Discard any excess marinade.

### Variation

Use 4 boneless, skinless chicken breasts or 8 chicken thighs in place of shrimp. Grill on high for 5 to 6 minutes, or until chicken is no longer pink inside and reaches an internal temperature of 170°F (75°C).

# Main Entrées: Pork, Lamb and Veal

Blackened Pork Chops . . . . . . . . . . . . . . . . . . . . . . . . . . 156

Breaded Pork Chops on the Grill . . . . . . . . . . . . . . . . . 157

Chinese-Style Pork . . . . . . . . . . . . . . . . . . . . . . . . . . . 158

Maple-Glazed Pork Chops . . . . . . . . . . . . . . . . . . . . . . 159

Saucy Pork Chops. . . . . . . . . . . . . . . . . . . . . . . . . . . . 160

Teriyaki Pork Chops . . . . . . . . . . . . . . . . . . . . . . . . . . 161

Hawaiian-Style Pork . . . . . . . . . . . . . . . . . . . . . . . . . . 162

Sausage and Vegetable Herbed Pasta Toss . . . . . . . . . . 164

Sausage "Meatballs" . . . . . . . . . . . . . . . . . . . . . . . . . 166

Dijon Rosemary Lamb Chops . . . . . . . . . . . . . . . . . . . 167

Lamb Kofte with Tzatziki . . . . . . . . . . . . . . . . . . . . . . 168

Minty Grilled Lamb Chops . . . . . . . . . . . . . . . . . . . . . 169

Veal Marsala . . . . . . . . . . . . . . . . . . . . . . . . . . . . . . . 170

Veal Parmigiana . . . . . . . . . . . . . . . . . . . . . . . . . . . . 172

# Blackened Pork Chops

*Bring a little pizzazz to your pork chops with this plucky fusion recipe.*

If your contact grill has more than one temperature setting, set it to high for this recipe.

## Tips

Make your own Cajun Spice Blend (see recipe, page 135).

## Make Ahead

Prepare bread crumb mixture up to 1 day in advance. Cover and refrigerate.

| 6 tbsp | plum sauce | 90 mL |
| ¼ cup | dry bread crumbs | 50 mL |
| 3 tbsp | dried onion soup mix (about ½ envelope) | 45 mL |
| 2 tsp | Cajun spice seasoning | 10 mL |
| 8 | boneless pork loin chops | 8 |

**1.** Pour plum sauce into a small shallow bowl.

**2.** In a shallow dish, combine bread crumbs with onion soup mix and Cajun spice. Mix well.

**3.** Dip pork chops in plum sauce and then roll in bread crumbs, coating evenly. Discard any excess plum sauce and crumb mixture. Place pork in a shallow dish, cover and refrigerate for a minimum of 20 minutes or for up to 1 hour. Meanwhile, preheat contact grill.

**4.** Spray both sides of contact grill with vegetable cooking spray or oil. Place pork on grill, close lid and grill for 6 to 8 minutes, or until just a hint of pink remains in pork and internal temperature reaches 160°F (71°C) and coating is blackened.

### Variation
Use 4 boneless, skinless chicken breasts in place of pork chops. Grill on high for 5 to 6 minutes, or until chicken is no longer pink inside and reaches an internal temperature of 170°F (75°C).

# Breaded Pork Chops on the Grill

**SERVES 4**

*Prepare traditional breaded pork chops on the grill the lower-fat way.*

If your contact grill has more than one temperature setting, set it to high for this recipe.

## Tips
You can grill the pork chops immediately after breading, but for best results refrigerate for 20 minutes before grilling so the breading has a chance to set.

## Make Ahead
Prepare bread crumb mixture up to 1 day in advance. Cover and refrigerate.

| | | |
|---|---|---|
| ½ cup | dry bread crumbs | 125 mL |
| 1 tsp | dried thyme | 5 mL |
| 1 tsp | dried parsley flakes | 5 mL |
| 1 tsp | seasoned salt (see tip, page 26) | 5 mL |
| ½ tsp | garlic powder | 2 mL |
| ½ tsp | freshly ground black pepper | 2 mL |
| 8 | boneless pork loin chops | 8 |
| 1 | egg | 1 |

1. In a shallow dish, combine bread crumbs with thyme, parsley, seasoned salt, garlic powder and pepper. In a separate shallow dish, lightly beat egg to loosen.

2. Dip pork chops in egg and then roll in bread crumbs, coating evenly. Discard any excess egg and crumb mixture. Place pork in a shallow dish, cover and refrigerate for a minimum of 20 minutes. Meanwhile, preheat contact grill.

3. Spray both sides of contact grill with vegetable cooking spray or oil. Place pork on grill, close lid and grill for 6 to 8 minutes, or until just a hint of pink remains in pork and internal temperature reaches 160°F (71°C) and coating is crispy.

### Variation
Use corn flakes crumbs in place of bread crumbs for a different flavor.

# Chinese-Style Pork

*Boneless pork chops are ideal for the grill, and they shine in this recipe.*

If your contact grill has more than one temperature setting, set it to high for this recipe.

**Tip**
Fresh gingerroot makes a big difference in this dish. If it's not available, use ¼ tsp (1 mL) ground ginger instead.

**Make Ahead**
Prepare marinade up to 1 day in advance. Cover and refrigerate.

| | | |
|---|---|---|
| 1 tsp | peanut oil | 5 mL |
| 3 | cloves garlic, minced | 3 |
| 2 | green onions, minced | 2 |
| 1 tsp | minced gingerroot | 5 mL |
| ⅓ cup | soy sauce | 75 mL |
| 3 tbsp | hoisin sauce | 45 mL |
| 2 tbsp | packed brown sugar | 25 mL |
| 1 tbsp | oyster sauce | 15 mL |
| 1 tbsp | sherry | 15 mL |
| ¼ tsp | Chinese five-spice powder (see tip, page 94) | 1 mL |
| 8 | boneless pork loin chops | 8 |

1. In a small saucepan, heat oil over medium heat. Sauté garlic, green onions and gingerroot for 3 minutes, until softened. Add soy sauce, hoisin sauce, brown sugar, oyster sauce, sherry and Chinese five-spice and bring to a boil over medium heat. Reduce heat to medium-low and simmer for 5 minutes, stirring, until marinade is the consistency of syrup. Let cool to room temperature.

2. Place pork in a shallow dish and brush with marinade, coating evenly. Cover and refrigerate for a minimum of 20 minutes or for up to 1 hour. Meanwhile, preheat contact grill.

3. Spray both sides of contact grill with vegetable cooking spray or oil. Place pork on grill, close lid and grill for 5 to 8 minutes, or until just a hint of pink remains in pork and internal temperature reaches 160°F (71°C).

**Variation**
Use 4 boneless, skinless chicken breasts in place of pork chops. Grill on high for 5 to 6 minutes, or until chicken is no longer pink inside and reaches an internal temperature of 170°F (75°C).

# Maple-Glazed Pork Chops

*Maple-infused pork chops produce a sweet and savory main dish.*

| | | |
|---|---|---:|
| 3 | cloves garlic, minced | 3 |
| ¼ cup | pure maple syrup | 50 mL |
| ¼ cup | dark beer | 50 mL |
| ½ tsp | salt | 2 mL |
| ¼ tsp | freshly ground black pepper | 1 mL |
| 8 | boneless pork loin chops | 8 |

If your contact grill has more than one temperature setting, set it to high for this recipe.

1. In a small bowl, stir together garlic, maple syrup, beer, salt and pepper.
2. Place pork in a shallow dish and brush with marinade, coating evenly. Cover and refrigerate for a minimum of 20 minutes. Meanwhile, preheat contact grill.
3. Spray both sides of contact grill with vegetable cooking spray or oil. Place pork on grill, close lid and grill for 5 to 8 minutes, or until just a hint of pink remains in pork and internal temperature reaches 160°F (71°C).

**Tip**

For the best flavor, use an intense dark beer.

**Make Ahead**

Prepare marinade up to 1 day in advance. Cover and refrigerate.

### Variation

Use 4 boneless, skinless chicken breasts in place of pork chops. Grill on high for 5 to 6 minutes, or until chicken is no longer pink inside and reaches an internal temperature of 170°F (75°C).

# Saucy Pork Chops

*This dish is perfect for a busy workday — and no one will know how easy it is to whip up!*

If your contact grill has more than one temperature setting, set it to high for this recipe.

### Tip
To give the marinade more zing, use spicy ketchup or add ¼ tsp (1 mL) hot pepper flakes.

### Make Ahead
Prepare marinade up to 1 day in advance. Cover and refrigerate.

| | | |
|---|---|---:|
| ⅓ cup | ketchup | 75 mL |
| ¼ cup | packed brown sugar | 50 mL |
| ¼ cup | white vinegar | 50 mL |
| 2 tsp | dried onion flakes | 10 mL |
| 1 tsp | Worcestershire sauce | 5 mL |
| ½ tsp | garlic powder | 2 mL |
| ½ tsp | salt | 2 mL |
| ¼ tsp | freshly ground black pepper | 1 mL |
| 8 | boneless pork loin chops | 8 |

1. In a small saucepan, over medium heat, stir together ketchup, brown sugar, vinegar, onion flakes, Worcestershire, garlic powder, salt and pepper and bring to a boil. Reduce heat to medium-low and simmer for 5 minutes, stirring, until marinade has thickened. Let cool to room temperature.

2. Place pork in a shallow dish and brush with marinade, coating evenly. Cover and refrigerate for a minimum of 20 minutes or for up to 1 day. Meanwhile, preheat contact grill.

3. Spray both sides of contact grill with vegetable cooking spray or oil. Place pork on grill, close lid and grill for 5 to 8 minutes, or until just a hint of pink remains in pork and internal temperature reaches 160°F (71°C).

### Variation
Use 4 boneless, skinless chicken breasts in place of pork chops. Grill on high for 5 to 6 minutes, or until chicken is no longer pink inside and reaches an internal temperature of 170°F (75°C).

Lamb Kofte with Tzatziki (page 168)

# Teriyaki Pork Chops

*Serve this Asian-inspired recipe with sticky rice and grilled or stir-fried vegetables for a palate-pleasing dinner.*

If your contact grill has more than one temperature setting, set it to high for this recipe.

## Tip

For a mellower taste, use an equal amount of liquid honey in place of brown sugar.

## Make Ahead

Prepare marinade up to 1 day in advance. Cover and refrigerate.

| | | |
|---|---|---|
| 1 tsp | vegetable oil | 5 mL |
| 2 | cloves garlic, minced | 2 |
| 1 tsp | minced gingerroot | 5 mL |
| ¼ cup | soy sauce | 50 mL |
| 2 tbsp | packed brown sugar | 25 mL |
| 1 tbsp | freshly squeezed lemon juice | 15 mL |
| 1 tbsp | sherry | 15 mL |
| 8 | boneless pork loin chops | 8 |

1. In a small saucepan, heat oil over medium heat. Sauté garlic and gingerroot for 1 minute. Stir in soy sauce, brown sugar, lemon juice and sherry and bring to a boil. Reduce heat to medium-low and simmer for 5 minutes, stirring, until marinade has thickened. Let cool completely.

2. Place pork in a shallow dish and brush with marinade, coating evenly. Cover and refrigerate for a minimum of 20 minutes or for up to 1 hour. Meanwhile, preheat contact grill.

3. Spray both sides of contact grill with vegetable cooking spray or oil. Place pork on grill, close lid and grill for 5 to 8 minutes, or until just a hint of pink remains in pork and internal temperature reaches 160°F (71°C).

### Variation

Use 4 boneless, skinless chicken breasts in place of pork chops. Grill on high for 5 to 6 minutes, or until chicken is no longer pink inside and reaches an internal temperature of 170°F (75°C).

Grilled Bananas (page 177)

# Hawaiian-Style Pork

**SERVES 4**

*Fruit and pork marry well, especially in this easy-to-prepare dish.*

If your contact grill has more than one temperature setting, set it to high for this recipe.

**Tip**

I like unsweetened coconut for this dish because it's sweet enough with the pineapple juice and brown sugar. To toast coconut, place on baking sheet and bake in 350°F (180°C) oven for 2 to 3 minutes, or until golden. Watch carefully.

**Make Ahead**

Prepare marinade up to 1 day in advance. Cover and refrigerate.

| | | |
|---|---|---|
| 1 | can (14 oz/398 mL) pineapple tidbits | 1 |
| 1 tsp | vegetable oil | 5 mL |
| 2 | cloves garlic, minced | 2 |
| 1/3 cup | ketchup | 75 mL |
| 1/4 cup | packed brown sugar | 50 mL |
| 2 tbsp | cider vinegar | 25 mL |
| 8 | boneless pork loin chops | 8 |

**Hawaiian Sauce**

| | | |
|---|---|---|
| 1 tsp | cornstarch | 5 mL |
| 2 tsp | vegetable oil | 10 mL |
| 1 | clove garlic, minced | 1 |
| 1/2 | green bell pepper | 1/2 |
| 1/2 | onion, minced | 1/2 |
| 1 tbsp | packed brown sugar | 15 mL |
| 1 tbsp | cider vinegar | 15 mL |
| 1 tbsp | toasted unsweetened coconut (see tip, at left) | 15 mL |

1. Drain pineapple, reserving juice. Set 1/2 cup (125 mL) tidbits and 1 cup + 1 tbsp (265 mL) juice aside (reserve remaining tidbits for another use).

2. In a small saucepan, heat oil over medium heat. Sauté garlic for 1 minute, until softened. Stir in ketchup, brown sugar, cider vinegar and 1/2 cup (125 mL) reserved pineapple juice and bring to a boil over medium heat. Reduce heat to medium-low and simmer for 5 minutes, stirring, until sugar is dissolved and marinade has thickened. Let cool completely.

**3.** Place pork in a shallow dish and brush with marinade, coating evenly. Cover and refrigerate for a minimum of 20 minutes or for up to 1 hour. Meanwhile, preheat contact grill.

**4.** *Prepare Hawaiian Sauce:* In a small bowl, whisk together cornstarch and 1 tbsp (15 mL) reserved pineapple juice. Set aside. In a medium saucepan, heat oil over medium heat. Sauté garlic, pepper and onion for 3 minutes, until softened. Stir in pineapple tidbits, $\frac{1}{2}$ cup (125 mL) reserved pineapple juice, brown sugar and vinegar and bring to a boil over medium heat. Stir cornstarch mixture into sauce. Reduce heat to medium-low and simmer for 5 minutes, stirring, until sauce is thickened. Just before serving, add coconut.

**5.** Spray both sides of contact grill with vegetable cooking spray or oil. Place pork on grill, close lid and grill for 5 to 8 minutes, or until just a hint on pink remains in pork and internal temperature reaches 160°F (71°C). Top grilled pork chops with sauce.

### Variation
Use 4 boneless, skinless chicken breasts in place of pork chops. Grill on high for 5 to 6 minutes, or until chicken is no longer pink inside and reaches an internal temperature of 170°F (75°C).

# Sausage and Vegetable Herbed Pasta Toss

*Soft Italian sausages lose the fat, but not the flavor, when grilled. Paired with grilled vegetables, this pasta dish will delight both family and guests.*

If your contact grill has more than one temperature setting, set it to high for this recipe.

### Tip
Fresh herbs make a big difference in this dish. Try to use them if possible.

### Make Ahead
Slice vegetables up to 8 hours in advance and prepare marinade up to 1 day in advance. Cover and refrigerate.

| | | |
|---|---|---|
| 2 | cloves garlic, minced | 2 |
| 1/4 cup | dry white wine | 50 mL |
| 2 tbsp | olive oil | 25 mL |
| 1 tbsp | chopped fresh oregano (or 1 tsp/5 mL dried) | 15 mL |
| 1 tbsp | chopped fresh thyme (or 1 tsp/5 mL dried) | 15 mL |
| 1 tbsp | chopped fresh basil (or 1 tsp/5 mL dried) | 15 mL |
| 1/2 tsp | kosher salt | 2 mL |
| 1/4 tsp | freshly ground black pepper | 1 mL |
| 1 | zucchini, sliced in rounds | 1 |
| 1 | onion, quartered | 1 |
| 1/2 | red bell pepper, cut into chunks | 1/2 |
| 1/2 | green bell pepper, cut into chunks | 1/2 |
| 2 cups | mushrooms, halved (about 8 oz/250 g) | 500 mL |
| 1 lb | soft Italian sausages | 500 g |
| 12 oz | rotini pasta | 375 g |
| | Freshly grated Parmesan cheese | |

1. In a small bowl, whisk together garlic, white wine, olive oil, oregano, thyme, basil, salt and pepper. Measure out half of the marinade and brush on zucchini, onion, red pepper, green pepper and mushrooms, tossing to ensure vegetables are well coated. Set aside.

2. Split sausages lengthwise and place cut-side down on preheated grill. Close lid and grill for 12 minutes, or until no longer pink and cooked through.

3. Meanwhile, cook pasta in boiling salted water for 8 minutes, or until al dente. Drain. Place pasta in a large serving bowl.

4. When sausages are grilled through, remove from grill. Cut into chunks and add to pasta. Cover and keep warm.

5. Spray both sides of contact grill with vegetable cooking spray or oil. Grill onion and red and green peppers for 4 minutes, zucchini and mushrooms for 3 minutes or until soft.

6. Add vegetables to pasta and sausage. Drizzle remainder of marinade over pasta. Toss well and serve warm. Sprinkle with Parmesan cheese.

### Variations

Use Greek or chorizo sausage for a different flavor. Slice sausage lengthwise before grilling.

Add other vegetables such as broccoli, asparagus and eggplant to pasta toss. Grill broccoli for 10 minutes and asparagus spears and eggplant slices for 5 to 6 minutes.

# Sausage "Meatballs"

*Serve these grilled "meatballs" on top of spaghetti with tomato sauce or in a crusty Italian bun as a sandwich. No one will mind that they are slightly flattened!*

If your contact grill has more than one temperature setting, set it to high for this recipe.

**Tip**

Use your instant-read meat thermometer to make sure sausage is cooked through. If you don't have a thermometer, cut into a meatball to ensure they are thoroughly cooked.

**Make Ahead**

Prepare sausage "meatballs" up to 1 day in advance. Cover and refrigerate until ready to grill.

| | | |
|---|---|---|
| 1 lb | hot Italian sausages | 500 g |
| 1 | egg, beaten | 1 |
| 1 | clove garlic, minced | 1 |
| 1/3 cup | corn flakes crumbs | 75 mL |
| 1/4 cup | ketchup | 50 mL |
| 1 tbsp | dried onion flakes | 15 mL |
| 1/2 tsp | salt | 2 mL |
| 1/4 tsp | freshly ground black pepper | 1 mL |

1. Remove sausage from casings and crumble into a medium bowl. Add egg, garlic, corn flakes crumbs, ketchup, onion flakes, salt and pepper. Mix until well blended. Form into balls about 1 inch (2.5 cm) in diameter. Cover and refrigerate for a minimum of 20 minutes. Meanwhile, preheat contact grill.

2. Spray both sides of contact grill with vegetable cooking spray or oil. Place sausage balls on grill, close lid and grill for 8 to 10 minutes, or until sausage is no longer pink inside, juices run clear, and sausage reaches an internal temperature of 170°F (75°C).

**Variation**

For a milder dish, use half lean ground beef and half sausage.

# Dijon Rosemary Lamb Chops

*These succulent lamb chops invite accompaniments of mashed potatoes and asparagus.*

If your contact grill has more than one temperature setting, set it to high for this recipe.

**Make Ahead**

Prepare marinade up to 1 day in advance. Cover and refrigerate.

| | | |
|---|---|---|
| 2 tbsp | Dijon mustard | 25 mL |
| 1 tbsp | grainy mustard | 15 mL |
| 2 tsp | white wine vinegar | 10 mL |
| 1 tbsp | chopped fresh rosemary (or 1 tsp/5 mL dried) | 15 mL |
| 1/2 tsp | kosher salt | 2 mL |
| 1/2 tsp | garlic powder | 2 mL |
| 1/4 tsp | freshly ground black pepper | 1 mL |
| 8 | bone-in lamb chops (about 1 1/2 lb/750 g) | 8 |

1. In a small bowl, whisk together Dijon mustard, grainy mustard, vinegar, rosemary, salt, garlic powder and pepper.

2. Place lamb chops in a shallow dish and brush with marinade, coating evenly. Cover and refrigerate for a minimum of 20 minutes or for up to 1 hour. Meanwhile, preheat contact grill.

3. Spray both sides of contact grill with vegetable cooking spray or oil. Place lamb on grill, close lid and grill for 6 to 8 minutes, or until lamb reaches an internal temperature of 160°F (71°C) for medium or until desired doneness.

**Variation**
Use boneless lamb chops and decrease the grilling time to 5 to 7 minutes.

# Lamb Kofte with Tzatziki

**SERVES 4**

*No worries about the lamb kofte skewers falling through the grate when you turn to your indoor grill for this flavorful Middle East feast.*

If your contact grill has more than one temperature setting, set it to high for this recipe.

**Tip**

If you prefer, serve with tahini instead of tzatziki sauce.

**Make Ahead**

Prepare and assemble lamb koftes up to 8 hours in advance. Cover tightly with plastic wrap and refrigerate until ready to grill.

- Eight 9-inch (23 cm) bamboo skewers

| | | |
|---|---|---|
| 1 lb | lean ground lamb | 500 g |
| 3 | cloves garlic, minced | 3 |
| 1 | egg, beaten | 1 |
| 1/2 cup | dry bread crumbs | 125 mL |
| 1 tbsp | dried onion flakes | 15 mL |
| 1 tsp | ground cumin | 5 mL |
| 1 tsp | ground cardamom | 5 mL |
| 1 tsp | dried parsley flakes | 5 mL |
| 1/2 tsp | ground coriander | 2 mL |
| 1/2 tsp | kosher salt | 2 mL |
| 1/4 tsp | dried mint | 1 mL |
| 1/4 tsp | freshly ground black pepper | 1 mL |
| 4 | pitas, sliced in half crosswise | 4 |
| 1 | tomato, diced | 1 |
| 1/2 | green bell pepper, thinly sliced | 1/2 |
| 1/2 | red onion, sliced | 1/2 |
| | Tzatziki Sauce (see recipe, page 93) | |

1. Soak bamboo skewers in hot water for 20 minutes.

2. In a medium bowl, combine ground lamb with garlic, egg, bread crumbs, onion flakes, cumin, cardamom, parsley, coriander, salt, mint and pepper. Mix until well blended.

3. Form one-eighth of the lamb mixture into an elongated sausage shape and place lengthwise on a skewer, wrapping meat around skewer. Repeat until 8 lamb kofte skewers are formed. Place in a shallow dish, cover and refrigerate for a minimum of 20 minutes or for up to 1 day. Meanwhile, preheat contact grill.

4. Spray both sides of contact grill with vegetable cooking spray or oil. Place skewers on grill, close lid and grill for 7 to 9 minutes, or until lamb is no longer pink inside and reaches an internal temperature of 170°F (75°C).

5. Serve in pitas with tomatoes, peppers, onions and Tzatziki Sauce (see recipe, page 93).

# Minty Grilled Lamb Chops

*Boneless lamb chops grill more quickly than the more readily available bone-in lamb chops. Just ask your butcher to remove the bone.*

If your contact grill has more than one temperature setting, set it to high for this recipe.

### Tip
You may find it easier to spread this sticky marinade on with your hands.

### Make Ahead
Prepare marinade up to 1 day in advance. Cover and refrigerate.

| | | |
|---|---|---|
| 2 tbsp | mint jelly | 25 mL |
| $\frac{1}{2}$ tsp | dried rosemary (or 1$\frac{1}{2}$ tsp/7 mL fresh) | 2 mL |
| $\frac{1}{2}$ tsp | dried parsley flakes (or 1$\frac{1}{2}$ tsp/7 mL chopped fresh parsley) | 2 mL |
| $\frac{1}{2}$ tsp | dried mint (or 1$\frac{1}{2}$ tsp/7 mL chopped fresh) | 2 mL |
| $\frac{1}{2}$ tsp | kosher salt | 2 mL |
| $\frac{1}{4}$ tsp | garlic powder | 1 mL |
| $\frac{1}{4}$ tsp | freshly ground black pepper | 1 mL |
| 1 lb | boneless lamb chops | 500 g |

1. In a small microwave-safe bowl, microwave mint jelly, uncovered, on High for about 30 seconds, or until melted. Mix in rosemary, parsley, mint, salt, garlic powder and pepper.

2. Place lamb chops in a shallow dish and brush with marinade, coating evenly. Cover and refrigerate for a minimum of 20 minutes or for up to 1 hour. Meanwhile, preheat contact grill.

3. Spray both sides of contact grill with vegetable cooking spray or oil. Place lamb on grill, close lid and grill for 5 to 7 minutes, or until lamb reaches an internal temperature of 160°F (71°C) for medium or until desired doneness.

### Variation
Use 8 bone-in lamb chops (about 1$\frac{1}{2}$ lbs/750 g) and increase the grilling time to 6 to 8 minutes.

# Veal Marsala

*This is one of my favorite dishes to serve to company or to prepare for a special occasion. The grill makes it fast and delicious!*

If your contact grill has more than one temperature setting, set it to high for this recipe.

**Tip**
Marsala wine is a fortified wine from the Sicilian region in Italy and is ideal for cooking.

**Make Ahead**
Prepare Marsala Sauce up to 8 hours in advance. Cover and refrigerate. Reheat in microwave on Medium for 2 minutes, stirring several times, until heated through.

| | | |
|---|---|---|
| ½ cup | dry bread crumbs | 125 mL |
| 1 tsp | dried Italian seasoning | 5 mL |
| ½ tsp | kosher salt | 2 mL |
| ¼ tsp | freshly ground black pepper | 1 mL |
| ¼ tsp | garlic powder | 1 mL |
| 1 | egg | 1 |
| 4 | veal cutlets (about 1¼ lbs/625 g) | 4 |
| 1 | lemon, sliced | 1 |

**Marsala Sauce**

| | | |
|---|---|---|
| 1 tbsp | olive oil | 15 mL |
| 3 | cloves garlic, minced | 3 |
| 1 | onion, chopped | 1 |
| ½ | red bell pepper, sliced in strips | ½ |
| ½ | green bell pepper, sliced in strips | ½ |
| 1½ cups | sliced mushrooms, (about 4 oz/125 g) | 375 mL |
| 1 cup | marsala wine | 250 mL |
| ¼ tsp | dried thyme | 1 mL |
| ¼ tsp | salt | 1 mL |
| ¼ tsp | freshly ground black pepper | 1 mL |
| 1 | dried bay leaf | 1 |

1. In a shallow dish, combine bread crumbs with Italian seasoning, salt, pepper and garlic powder. In a separate shallow dish, lightly beat egg to loosen.

2. Dip each veal cutlet in egg and then in bread crumbs, coating evenly. Discard any excess egg and crumbs. Place veal in a shallow dish, cover and refrigerate for a minimum of 20 minutes or for up to 1 hour. Meanwhile, preheat contact grill.

**3.** *Prepare Marsala Sauce:* In a large skillet, heat olive oil over medium heat. Sauté garlic, onion, red pepper, green pepper and mushrooms for 5 to 7 minutes, or until tender. Add Marsala wine, thyme, salt, pepper and bay leaf, stirring well. Increase heat to high and bring to a boil. Reduce heat to medium-low and simmer for 10 minutes, uncovered, until sauce is reduced and thickened.

**4.** Meanwhile, spray both sides of contact grill with vegetable cooking spray or oil. Lightly spray both sides of each cutlet using a spray pump filled with olive oil or vegetable oil. Place cutlets on grill, close lid and grill for 6 to 8 minutes, or until coating is golden brown and veal is cooked through.

**5.** Remove veal cutlets from grill and add to Marsala sauce, stirring to cover cutlets well with vegetables and sauce. Serve with slices of fresh lemon.

### Variation
Use 4 chicken cutlets in place of veal cutlets and grill for 6 to 8 minutes, or until chicken is no longer pink inside and reaches an internal temperature of 170°F (75°C).

# Veal Parmigiana

*Breaded veal cutlets topped with mozzarella have returned as a comfort food worthy of our attention when they're prepared the fuss-free, lower-fat way on the grill. Serve with pasta and tomato sauce.*

If your contact grill has more than one temperature setting, set it to high for this recipe.

### Tip
Veal is a lean meat often overlooked as a good source of protein.

| | | |
|---|---|---|
| ½ cup | dry bread crumbs | 125 mL |
| ½ cup | freshly grated Parmesan cheese | 125 mL |
| ½ tsp | dried parsley flakes | 2 mL |
| ½ tsp | kosher salt | 2 mL |
| ¼ tsp | freshly ground black pepper | 1 mL |
| ¼ tsp | garlic powder | 1 mL |
| 1 | egg | 1 |
| 4 | veal cutlets (about 1¼ lbs/625 g) | 4 |
| ¾ cup | shredded skim mozzarella cheese | 175 mL |
| | Tomato sauce, heated (optional) | |

1. In a shallow dish, combine bread crumbs, Parmesan cheese, parsley, salt, pepper and garlic powder. In a separate shallow dish, lightly beat egg to loosen.

2. Dip each veal cutlet in egg and then in bread crumbs, coating evenly. Discard any excess egg and crumbs. Place veal in a shallow dish, cover and refrigerate for a minimum of 20 minutes or for up to 1 hour. Meanwhile, preheat contact grill.

3. Spray both sides of contact grill with vegetable cooking spray or oil. Lightly spray both sides of each cutlet using a spray pump filled with olive oil or vegetable oil. Place cutlets on grill, close lid and and grill for 6 to 8 minutes, or until coating is golden brown and veal is cooked through.

4. Leave cutlets on grill and sprinkle cheese equally on top of veal cutlets. Hold lid down (do not close entirely) for 1 to 2 minutes, or until cheese has melted.

5. Top veal cutlets with tomato sauce, if desired, just before serving.

### Variation
Use 6 chicken cutlets in place of veal cutlets and grill for 6 to 8 minutes, or until chicken is no longer pink inside and reaches an internal temperature of 170°F (75°C).

# Desserts

Angel Food Cake and Fruit Kabobs . . . . . . . . . . . . . . . 174

Black Forest Pound Cake . . . . . . . . . . . . . . . . . . . . . 175

Caramel Pound Cake . . . . . . . . . . . . . . . . . . . . . . 176

Grilled Bananas . . . . . . . . . . . . . . . . . . . . . . . . . 177

Grilled Brie Pockets. . . . . . . . . . . . . . . . . . . . . . . 178

Grilled Fruit Kabobs . . . . . . . . . . . . . . . . . . . . . . 179

Just Like Campfire S'mores. . . . . . . . . . . . . . . . . . 180

Tortilla S'mores. . . . . . . . . . . . . . . . . . . . . . . . . 181

# Angel Food Cake and Fruit Kabobs

*This combination of grilled angel food cake covered in a maple sauce is reminiscent of pancakes with syrup and is simply irresistible.*

If your contact grill has more than one temperature setting, set it to high for this recipe.

**Tip**
If the strawberries are extra large, slice them into quarters.

- Eight 9-inch (23 cm) bamboo skewers

| | | |
|---|---|---|
| ½ | angel food cake (from a mix or homemade), cut into 1-inch (2.5 cm) cubes (about 4 cups/1 L) | ½ |
| 1 lb | strawberries, halved (about 4 cups/1 L) | 500 g |
| 1 cup | blueberries (about 4 oz/125 g) | 250 mL |

**Sauce**

| | | |
|---|---|---|
| ½ cup | pure maple syrup | 125 mL |
| ½ cup | unsweetened pineapple juice | 125 mL |
| Pinch | ground cloves | Pinch |

1. Soak bamboo skewers in hot water for 30 minutes. Drain and pat dry.

2. *Prepare sauce:* In a small bowl, stir together maple syrup, pineapple juice and cloves.

3. Prepare kabobs by threading cake cubes, strawberry halves and blueberries alternately onto skewers. Place kabobs in a shallow dish and brush sauce over fruit kabobs, turning several times to coat evenly.

4. Spray both sides of contact grill with vegetable spray or oil. Place kabobs on grill, close lid and grill for 1 to 2 minutes, or until cake is crisped and fruit is softened but not mushy.

**Variation**
Add or substitute any fruits you prefer in place of the blueberries, such as bananas, pear chunks or apple chunks.

# Black Forest Pound Cake

*This dessert has all the components of delicious Black Forest cake — chocolate, cherries, whipping cream — but is a breeze to prepare on your indoor grill.*

If your contact grill has more than one temperature setting, set it to high for this recipe.

## Tip

For best results, place beaters and bowl in the freezer for 30 minutes before whipping cream.

| 1 cup | whipping (35%) cream | 250 mL |
|---|---|---|
| 8 | maraschino cherries, quartered | 8 |
| 8 | slices ($1/2$ inch/1 cm thick) pound cake (about 1 lb/500 g) | 8 |
| 48 | semi-sweet chocolate chips | 48 |
| | Additional maraschino cherries (optional) | |

1. In a mixing bowl, on high speed, whip cream until firm peaks form. Cover and refrigerate until ready to use.

2. Using your hands, press 4 maraschino cherry pieces into each slice of pound cake. Flip over and press in 6 chocolate chips.

3. Spray both sides of contact grill with vegetable cooking spray or oil. Place pound cake slices on grill, close lid and grill for 3 minutes, until cake is golden brown.

4. Serve each piece of pound cake with a dollop of whipped cream and additional maraschino cherries, if desired.

### Variation

Use white chocolate chips and dried cranberries in place of semi-sweet chocolate chips and maraschino cherries.

# Caramel Pound Cake

**SERVES 8**

*Grilled caramel pound cake is a decadent dessert — and it's even better when served with maple walnut or vanilla ice cream and fresh fruit.*

If your contact grill has more than one temperature setting, set it to high for this recipe.

| | | |
|---|---|---|
| ¹⁄₄ cup | packed dark brown sugar | 50 mL |
| ¹⁄₄ cup | butter | 50 mL |
| ¹⁄₄ cup | coffee-flavored liqueur | 50 mL |
| 8 | slices (¹⁄₂ inch/1 cm thick) pound cake (about 1 lb/500 g) | 8 |

1. In a small saucepan, over medium heat, stir brown sugar and butter together until sugar is dissolved, about 1 to 2 minutes. Remove from heat and slowly add liqueur (stand back because liqueur will sizzle).

2. In a shallow dish, brush sauce on pound cake slices, turning several times to coat evenly.

3. Spray both sides of contact grill with vegetable cooking spray or oil. Place pound cake slices on grill, close lid and grill for 3 minutes, until cake is golden brown.

**Variation**
Use orange-flavored liqueur in place of coffee-flavored.

# Grilled Bananas

*Not unlike Mexican fried bananas, this dessert reaches another luscious level when topped with vanilla ice cream, chocolate sauce and walnuts.*

If your contact grill has more than one temperature setting, set it to high for this recipe.

| 3 tbsp | packed brown sugar | 45 mL |
| 2 tbsp | butter | 25 mL |
| 1 tbsp | orange-flavored liqueur | 15 mL |
| 2 tsp | freshly squeezed lemon juice | 10 mL |
| 1/4 tsp | ground cinnamon | 1 mL |
| 4 | bananas, peeled and sliced in half lengthwise | 4 |

1. In a small saucepan, over medium heat, stir brown sugar and butter together until butter is melted. Add liqueur, lemon juice and cinnamon. Continue stirring until sugar is dissolved. Remove from heat and let cool to room temperature.

2. Place sliced bananas in a shallow dish. Pour sauce over bananas, turning the fruit to coat evenly.

3. Spray both sides of contact grill with vegetable cooking spray or oil. Place bananas on contact grill, close lid and grill for 2 minutes, until fruit is softened but not mushy.

### Variation
Use almond-flavored liqueur in place of orange-flavored.

# Grilled Brie Pockets

*Brie is good anytime, but especially when melted with a sugary pecan syrup and sandwiched between slices of angel food cake.*

If your contact grill has more than one temperature setting, set it to high for this recipe.

| | | |
|---|---|---|
| ¹⁄₂ | angel food cake (from a mix or homemade, about 8 oz/250 g) | ¹⁄₂ |
| 4 oz | Brie cheese, cut into 4 slices | 125 g |
| ¹⁄₂ cup | packed brown sugar | 125 mL |
| 1 tbsp | rum | 15 mL |
| ¹⁄₄ cup | chopped pecans | 50 mL |

1. Cut angel food cake into 4 thick slices, then cut each slice in half crosswise to make 2 layers. Place a slice of Brie on each bottom piece.

2. In a small saucepan, over medium heat, bring brown sugar, rum and 1 tbsp (15 mL) water to a boil, stirring constantly, until sugar is dissolved. Add pecans, stirring to coat.

3. Dividing pecan sauce evenly, brush sauce on each Brie slice. Place remaining cake pieces on top, making sandwiches, and squish down.

4. Spray both sides of contact grill with vegetable cooking spray or oil. Place cake sandwiches on grill, close lid and grill for 1 to 2 minutes, or until cake is crispy and golden and Brie is melted. Serve warm.

**Variation**
Use walnuts in place of pecans.

# Grilled Fruit Kabobs

SERVES 8

*This dessert wins top marks for easy preparation and a sinfully sweet and spicy syrup.*

If your contact grill has more than one temperature setting, set it to high for this recipe.

## Tips

Add or substitute any fruits you prefer, such as apple chunks, strawberries or banana slices.

Enticingly aromatic, vanilla sugar can be found at specialty food stores. Vanilla beans are packed in with granulated sugar for about a week and then removed. The essence of vanilla remains and gives the sugar a fabulous vanilla flavor.

- *Eight 9-inch (23 cm) bamboo skewers*

| | | |
|---|---|---|
| 1½ cups | fresh or canned pineapple chunks | 375 mL |
| 1 | pear, cut into ½-inch (1 cm) cubes | 1 |
| ¼ cup | halved drained maraschino cherries | 50 mL |
| **Sauce** | | |
| ½ cup | unsweetened pineapple juice | 125 mL |
| ¼ cup | vanilla sugar | 50 mL |
| ¼ cup | coconut-flavored rum | 50 mL |
| Pinch | ground cinnamon | Pinch |
| Pinch | ground cardamom | Pinch |
| Pinch | ground nutmeg | Pinch |

1. Soak bamboo skewers in hot water for 30 minutes.

2. *Prepare sauce:* In a small saucepan, over medium heat, bring pineapple juice, vanilla sugar, rum, cinnamon, cardamom and nutmeg to a boil, stirring constantly. Remove from heat and let cool to room temperature.

3. Prepare kabobs by threading pineapple chunks, pear cubes and maraschino cherry halves alternately onto skewers. Place kabobs in a shallow dish and brush sauce over kabobs, turning several times to coat evenly.

4. Spray both sides of contact grill with vegetable cooking spray or oil. Place kabobs on contact grill, close lid and grill for 2 to 3 minutes, or until fruit is softened but not mushy.

# Just Like Campfire S'mores

**SERVES 4**

*For those who shudder at the thought of messing with the traditional graham wafer treat, here's a way to capture the essence of campfire s'mores, minus the campfire.*

If your contact grill has more than one temperature setting, set it to high for this recipe.

**Tip**

Peanut butter and chocolate sauce help hold s'mores together on the indoor grill.

| | | |
|---|---|---|
| 4 tsp | smooth peanut butter | 20 mL |
| 8 | graham wafers (2- by 2-inch/5 by 5 cm) | 8 |
| 16 | miniature marshmallows | 16 |
| 4 tsp | chocolate sauce | 20 mL |

**1.** Spread 1 tsp (5 mL) peanut butter on each of 4 graham wafers, leaving a $\frac{1}{4}$-inch (5 mm) border around edge. Sprinkle with 4 marshmallows.

**2.** Spread chocolate sauce on each of the remaining 4 graham wafers, leaving a $\frac{1}{4}$-inch (5 mm) border around edge. Place chocolate-side down on top of the peanut butter and marshmallows. Press firmly to close.

**3.** Spray both sides of contact grill with vegetable cooking spray or oil. Place s'mores on grill, close lid gently and grill for 30 to 60 seconds, until marshmallows are melted.

**Variation**

Use 3 tbsp (45 mL) hazelnut chocolate spread in place of chocolate sauce and peanut butter.

# Tortilla S'mores

*You don't have to wait for the campfire to indulge in the all-time favorite camping treat. Your indoor grill makes it fast and easy, with no worries about burning your fingertips!*

If your contact grill has more than one temperature setting, set it to high for this recipe.

| 4 | 7-inch (18 cm) tortillas | 4 |
| 4 | graham wafers (2- by 2-inch/5 by 5 cm) | 4 |
| 56 | miniature marshmallows | 56 |
| 1/4 cup | semi-sweet chocolate chips | 50 mL |

1. Lay tortillas on a flat work surface. Coarsely crumble one graham wafer at a time by hand and sprinkle over each tortilla, covering one half of the surface. Top with 14 marshmallows and sprinkle with chocolate chips. Fold tortillas over to create half moons.

2. Spray both sides of contact grill with vegetable cooking spray or oil. Place tortillas on grill with the open side facing the top edge, close lid and grill for 2 to 3 minutes, or until tortillas are crispy and golden and chocolate chips are partially melted.

3. Cut into triangles and serve.

### Variations
Try this recipe with whole wheat tortillas. Use butterscotch chips in place of chocolate chips.

**National Library of Canada Cataloguing in Publication**

Simon, Ilana, 1963-
    125 best indoor grill recipes / Ilana Simon.

Includes index.
ISBN 0-7788-0102-0

    1. Barbecue cookery.  I. Title.  II. Title: One hundred
twenty-five best indoor grill recipes.

TX840.B3S555 2004          641.7'6          C2004-902891-X

# Index

*Page references in italics indicate that the ingredient may be found in a variation.*

## A

All-in-One Cheeseburgers, 69
Angel Food Cake and Fruit Kabobs, 174
appetizers, 16–34
Asiago cheese
  Cheesy Turkey Burgers, 84
  Salami and Red Pepper Panini with Asiago, 60
Asian Steak Noodle Salad, 36
asparagus
  Beef Rollups with Asparagus and Goat Cheese, 22
  Grilled Asparagus, 46
  Grilled Cheese and Asparagus Rolls, 52
  Sausage and Vegetable Herbed Pasta Toss, *165*

## B

Baba Ghanouj, Grilled Eggplant, 16
bacon
  Bacon-Wrapped Scallops, 25
  Chicken Caesar Salad (tip), 38
bananas
  Angel Food Cake and Fruit Kabobs, 174
  Grilled Bananas, 177
Barbecued Chicken with a Difference, 108
Barbecued Steak, 96
beans
  Chicken and Bean Burritos, 114
  Tex-Mex Pasta Salad, 40
beef, 14, 90–106. *See also* veal
  All-in-One Cheeseburgers, 69

Asian Steak Noodle Salad, 36
Barbecued Steak, 96
Beef Rollups with Asparagus and Goat Cheese, 22
Beef Souvlaki, 92
Beer-Basted Beef, 91
Burgers with Horseradish and Caramelized Onions, 76
Caesar Burgers, 71
Curry Beef Burgers, 74
Fajitas, 98
French Quarter Burgers, 72
Grilled Salisbury Steak, 104
hickory burgers, *82*
Hot and Smoky Beef, 90
Italian burgers, *78*
Mexican Steak, 103
Moroccan Steak, 106
Mushroom-Filled Beef Rollups, 20
Mustard-Infused Steak, 97
Pea Soup with Grilled Hot Dogs, 33
Pepper Steak, 102
Pita Fajitas, 100
Reuben Sandwiches, 56
Sausage Burgers, 79
"meatballs," *166*
Seasoned Beef Burgers, 70
Smoky Mexican Burgers, 73
Steak and Vegetable "Stir-Fry," 94
tarragon mustard burgers, *83*
Tex-Mex Pasta Salad, 40
Thai Curry Burgers, 75
Thai noodle salad, *45*
Ultimate Hamburger, 68

Beef Rollups with Asparagus and Goat Cheese, 22
Beef Souvlaki, 92
beef stock
  Lentil Soup with Grilled Garlic Sausage, 34
  Pea Soup with Grilled Hot Dogs, 33
beer
  Beer-Basted Beef, 91
  Maple-Glazed Pork Chops, 159
  Mustard-Infused Steak, 97
Beer-Basted Beef, 91
Blackened Pork Chops, 156
Blackened Red Fish, 134
Black Forest Pound Cake, 175
Breaded Pork Chops on the Grill, 157
Brie cheese
  Grilled Brie Pockets, 178
  Grilled Mango and Brie Quesadillas, 63
broccoli
  Grilled Chicken Cacciatore, 118
  Grilled Vegetables, 48
  Sausage and Vegetable Herbed Pasta Toss, *165*
  Steak and Vegetable "Stir-Fry," 94
  Tempura Shrimp and Vegetables, 30
Bruschetta, Wild Mushroom, 18
burgers, 68
Burgers with Horseradish and Caramelized Onions, 76
Burritos, Chicken and Bean, 114
buttermilk
  Chicken Nuggets, *112*
  Southern "Fried" Chicken, 111

# C

Caesar Burgers, 71
Cajun Spice Blend, 134
cake
  Angel Food Cake and
    Fruit Kabobs, 174
  Black Forest Pound Cake,
    175
  Caramel Pound Cake,
    176
  Grilled Brie Pockets,
    178
Caramelized Onions, 77
Caramel Pound Cake, 176
carrots
  Lentil Soup with Grilled
    Garlic Sausage, 34
  Pea Soup with Grilled
    Hot Dogs, 33
  Thai Chicken Noodle
    Salad, 44
catfish
  blackened, *134*
  "Fried" Catfish, 136
cauliflower
  Grilled Chicken
    Cacciatore, 118
  Grilled Vegetables, 48
  Tempura Shrimp and
    Vegetables, 30
Cayenne Raspberry
  Chicken, 121
celery
  Lentil Soup with Grilled
    Garlic Sausage, 34
  Pea Soup with Grilled
    Hot Dogs, 33
Cheddar cheese
  Chicken and Bean
    Burritos, 114
  Grilled Cheese and
    Asparagus Rolls, 52
  Grilled Cheese
    Sandwich, 53
  Mexican Cheese
    Quesadillas, 64
  Tuna Melts #1, 57
  Tuna Melts #2, 58
cheese. *See also specific
    cheeses*
  All-in-One
    Cheeseburgers, 69
  Green Peppercorn and
    Gruyère Turkey Fillets,
    131

Italian Vegetable and
  Orzo Salad, 42
Three-Meat Panini with
  Provolone, 62
Cheesy Turkey Burgers,
  84
cherries, maraschino
  Black Forest Pound Cake,
    175
  Grilled Fruit Kabobs,
    179
chèvre (goat cheese)
  Beef Rollups with
    Asparagus and Goat
    Cheese, 22
  Crostini with Grilled
    Eggplant and Chèvre,
    17
chicken, 14, 108–30
  all-in-one cheeseburgers,
    *69*
  Asian noodle salad, *37*
  Barbecued Chicken with
    a Difference, 108
  blackened, *156*
  burgers with horseradish
    and caramelized
    onions, *76*
  Cayenne Raspberry
    Chicken, 121
  cheesy burgers, *84*
  Chicken and Bean
    Burritos, 114
  Chicken and Monterey
    Jack Quesadillas, 65
  Chicken Caesar Salad,
    38
  Chicken Nuggets, 112
  Chicken Shish Kabobs,
    23
  Chinese-style, *158*
  Cilantro Lime Chicken,
    124
  Coconut Mango
    Chicken Breasts, 123
  fajitas, *99*
  Four-Ingredient
    Chicken, 120
  Ginger, Soy and Lime
    Chicken, 125
  Greek Lemon Chicken,
    115
  Grilled Chicken
    Cacciatore, 118
  Hawaiian-style, *163*

Hickory Chicken
  Burgers, 82
Jerk Chicken, 110
lemon herb, *150*
mango burgers, *87*
Mango Chicken, 122
maple-glazed, *159*
Marsala, *171*
Moroccan, *151*
orange rosemary, *132*
Orange Sesame Chicken,
  126
Parmigiana, *172*
Pesto Chicken Thighs,
  116
saucy, *160*
satay, *29*
Singapore, *152*
Southern "Fried"
  Chicken, 111
Sticky Sesame Chicken,
  129
Szechuan Chicken, 128
Tarragon Mustard
  Chicken Burgers, 83
Teriyaki Chicken, 130,
  *161*
Tex-Mex Pasta Salad, *41*
Thai, *154*
Thai Chicken Noodle
  Salad, 44
Thai Curry Burgers, *75*
thyme burgers, *88*
ultimate burger, *68*
Weekday Barbecued
  Chicken, 109
Chicken and Bean
  Burritos, 114
Chicken and Monterey
  Jack Quesadillas, 65
Chicken Caesar Salad, 38
Chicken Nuggets, 112
Chicken Shish Kabobs,
  23
chilies
  Chicken and Bean
    Burritos, 114
  Chipotle Chili–Spiked
    Shrimp, 28
  Pita Fajitas, 100
  Smoky Mexican Burgers,
    73
Chinese-Style Breaded Veal
  Nuggets, 24
Chinese-Style Pork, 158

Chipotle Chili–Spiked Shrimp, 28
chocolate
  Black Forest Pound Cake, 175
  Just Like Campfire S'mores, 180
  Tortilla S'mores, 181
Cilantro Lime Chicken, 124
coconut
  Coconut Mango Chicken Breasts, 123
  Hawaiian-Style Pork, 162
Coconut Mango Chicken Breasts, 123
coconut milk
  Coconut Mango Chicken Breasts, 123
  Thai Curry Burgers, 75
  Thai Shrimp, 154
Couscous, 127
Crab Cakes with Red Pepper Aïoli, 26
cream cheese
  Creamy Turkey Burgers, 85
  Jalapeño Poppers, 19
Creamy Turkey Burgers, 85
Crostini with Grilled Eggplant and Chèvre, 17
Croutons, Homemade, 39
Cumin Lemon Tuna Steaks, 143
Curry Beef Burgers, 74

**D**
desserts, 174–81
Dijon Rosemary Lamb Chops, 167
dressings
  Asian Steak Noodle Salad, 36
  Caesar Burgers, 71
  Italian Vegetable and Orzo Salad, 42
  Salami and Red Pepper Panini with Asiago, 60
  Tex-Mex Pasta Salad, 40
  Thai Chicken Noodle Salad, 44
dry rubs. *See* rubs

**E**
eggplant
  Crostini with Grilled Eggplant and Chèvre, 17
  Grilled Eggplant Baba Ghanouj, 16
  Sausage and Vegetable Herbed Pasta Toss, *165*
eggs
  Grilled French Toast, 54
  "Monterey" Cristo Sandwiches, 55

**F**
fajitas, 98, 100
fish, 9, 14, 134–49. *See also specific fish*
  Blackened Red Fish, 134
  Chicken Caesar Salad, 38
  Lemon-Pepper Fish Fillets, 138
Four-Ingredient Chicken, 120
French Quarter Burgers, 72
French Toast, Grilled, 54
"Fried" Catfish, 136
fruit. *See also specific fruits;* fruit, dried
  Angel Food Cake and Fruit Kabobs, 174
  Black Forest Pound Cake, 175
  Cayenne Raspberry Chicken, 121
  Grilled Fruit Kabobs, 179
fruit, dried
  Black Forest Pound Cake, *175*
  Couscous, 127

**G**
Ginger, Soy and Lime Chicken, 125
Gravy, Mushroom and Onion, 104
Greek Lemon Chicken, 115
Green Peppercorn and Gruyère Turkey Fillets, 131
Gremolata, 139
Grilled Asparagus, 46
Grilled Bananas, 177
Grilled Brie Pockets, 178

Grilled Cheese and Asparagus Rolls, 52
Grilled Cheese Sandwich, 53
Grilled Chicken Cacciatore, 118
Grilled Eggplant Baba Ghanouj, 16
Grilled French Toast, 54
Grilled Fruit Kabobs, 179
Grilled Mango and Brie Quesadillas, 63
Grilled Salisbury Steak, 104
Grilled Tofu, 47
Grilled Vegetables, 48

**H**
halibut
  cumin lemon, *143*
  Herbed Halibut, 137
  Oriental, *148*
ham
  "Monterey" Cristo Sandwiches, *55*
  and red pepper panini with Asiago, *60*
  Three-Meat Panini with Provolone, *62*
Hawaiian Sauce, 162
Hawaiian-Style Pork, 162
Herbed Halibut, 137
Hickory Chicken Burgers, 82
Homemade Croutons, 39
Honey Dill Salmon with Dijon, 144
Honey Dill Sauce, 113
Honey Orange Salmon with Thyme, 145
Hot and Smoky Beef, 90

**I**
indoor grilling, 10, 12–13
indoor grills, 9–10
  tips for using, 11–12
Italian Veal Burgers, 78, 139
Italian Vegetable and Orzo Salad, 42

**J**
Jalapeño Poppers, 19
Jerk Chicken, 110
Just Like Campfire S'mores, 180

## L

lamb, 14
  Dijon Rosemary Lamb
    Chops, 167
  Lamb Kofte with
    Tzatziki, 168
  Minty Grilled Lamb
    Chops, 169
Lamb Kofte with Tzatziki,
  168
Lemon Herb Shrimp, 150
Lemon Honey Dill
  Salmon, 146
Lemon-Pepper Fish Fillets,
  138
lemons
  Cumin Lemon Tuna
    Steaks, 143
  Lemon Honey Dill
    Salmon, 146
  Moroccan Shrimp, 151
  Mustard Lemon Herb
    Rainbow Trout, 141
Lentil Soup with Grilled
  Garlic Sausage, 34
limes
  Asian Steak Noodle
    Salad, 36
  Blackened Red Fish, 134
  Chicken and Bean
    Burritos, 114
  Cilantro Lime Chicken,
    124
  Fajitas, 98
  Ginger, Soy and Lime
    Chicken, 125
  Grilled Mango and Brie
    Quesadillas, 63
  Jerk Chicken, 110
  Lime Shrimp, Susie's,
    153
  Mexican Steak, 103
  Oriental Salmon Steaks,
    148
  Pita Fajitas, 100
  Spicy Shrimp, 32
  Thai Shrimp, 154
Lime Shrimp, Susie's, 153
liqueurs
  Caramel Pound Cake,
    176
  Grilled Bananas, 177
  Grilled French Toast, 54
Low-Fat Potato Pancakes,
  50

## M

mango
  Coconut Mango
    Chicken Breasts, 123
  Grilled Mango and Brie
    Quesadillas, 63
  Mango Chicken, 122
  Turkey Mango Burgers,
    87
Mango Chicken, 122
Maple-Glazed Pork Chops,
  159
Maple-Glazed Sausage
  Sandwiches, 59
maple syrup
  Angel Food Cake and
    Fruit Kabobs, 174
  Grilled French Toast, 54
  Maple-Glazed Pork
    Chops, 159
  Maple-Glazed Sausage
    Sandwiches, 59
marinades, 13
  for beef, 20–22, 36,
    90–95, 97–103
  for fish, 134–35, 137–38,
    141–48
  for lamb, 167, 169
  for pork, 158–65
  for poultry, 23, 108–9,
    111, 114–15, 121–30,
    132
  for seafood, 150,
    152–54
  for tofu, 47
  for vegetables, 46,
    48–49, 80–81, 118–19,
    164–65
Marsala Sauce, 170
marshmallows
  Just Like Campfire
    S'mores, 180
  Tortilla S'mores, 181
Mexican Cheese
  Quesadillas, 64
Mexican Steak, 103
Minty Grilled Lamb
  Chops, 169
"Monterey" Cristo
  Sandwiches, 55
Monterey Jack cheese
  Chicken and Bean
    Burritos, 114
  Chicken and Monterey
    Jack Quesadillas, 65

Mexican Cheese
  Quesadillas, 64
"Monterey" Cristo
  Sandwiches, 55
Moroccan Shrimp, 151
Moroccan Steak, 106
mozzarella cheese
  Pita Pizzas, 66
  Veal Parmigiana, 172
Mushroom and Onion
  Gravy, 104
Mushroom-Filled Beef
  Rollups, 20
mushrooms
  Asian Steak Noodle
    Salad, 36
  Chicken Shish Kabobs,
    23
  Fajitas, 98
  Grilled Chicken
    Cacciatore, 118
  Grilled Salisbury Steak,
    104
  Grilled Vegetables, 48
  Italian Vegetable and
    Orzo Salad, 42
  Mushroom-Filled Beef
    Rollups, 20
  Pita Fajitas, 100
  Pita Pizzas, 66
  Portobello Mushroom
    Burgers, 80
  Sausage and Vegetable
    Herbed Pasta Toss, 164
  Steak and Vegetable
    "Stir-Fry," 94
  Veal Marsala, 170
  Wild Mushroom
    Bruschetta, 18
Mustard-Infused Steak, 97
Mustard Lemon Herb
  Rainbow Trout, 141

## N

noodles. *See also* pasta
  dishes
  Asian Steak Noodle
    Salad, 36
  Thai Chicken Noodle
    Salad, 44
nuts
  Asian Steak Noodle
    Salad, 36
  Grilled Brie Pockets, 178
  Pesto, 117

# O

olives
  Couscous, *127*
  Italian Vegetable and
    Orzo Salad, *43*
  Pimiento Turkey Burgers,
    86
  Tex-Mex Pasta Salad, *41*
onions. *See also* shallots
  Asian Steak Noodle
    Salad, 36
  Beef Souvlaki, 92
  Burgers with Horseradish
    and Caramelized
    Onions, 76
  Chicken Shish Kabobs,
    23
  Fajitas, 98
  Grilled Chicken
    Cacciatore, 118
  Grilled Salisbury Steak,
    104
  Grilled Vegetables, 48
  Italian Vegetable and
    Orzo Salad, 42
  Lamb Kofte with
    Tzatziki, 168
  Lentil Soup with Grilled
    Garlic Sausage, 34
  Low-Fat Potato
    Pancakes, 50
  Pea Soup with Grilled
    Hot Dogs, 33
  Pita Fajitas, 100
  Portobello Mushroom
    Burgers, 80
  Salami and Red Pepper
    Panini with Asiago, 60
  Sausage and Vegetable
    Herbed Pasta Toss,
    164
  Steak and Vegetable
    "Stir-Fry," 94
  Tex-Mex Pasta Salad, 40
  Veal Marsala, 170
Orange Rosemary Chicken
  Thighs, 132
oranges
  Couscous, 127
  Honey Orange Salmon
    with Thyme, 145
  Orange Rosemary
    Chicken Thighs, 132
  Orange Sesame Chicken,
    126

Orange Soy
  Ginger–Glazed
    Salmon, 147
  Szechuan Chicken, 128
Orange Sesame Chicken,
  126
Orange Soy Ginger–Glazed
  Salmon, 147
Oriental Salmon Steaks,
  148

# P

Pancakes, Low-Fat Potato,
  50
"Pan-Fried" Grilled
  Walleye, 140
Parmesan cheese
  Caesar Burgers, 71
  Chicken Caesar Salad,
    38
  Chicken Nuggets, 112
  Four-Ingredient
    Chicken, 120
  Pesto Chicken Thighs,
    116
  Portobello Mushroom
    Burgers, 80
  Southern "Fried"
    Chicken, 111
  Veal Parmigiana, 172
  Wild Mushroom
    Bruschetta, 18
pasta dishes. *See also*
  noodles
  Grilled Chicken
    Cacciatore, 118
  Italian Vegetable and
    Orzo Salad, 42
  Sausage and Vegetable
    Herbed Pasta Toss, 164
  Tex-Mex Pasta Salad, 40
pastes, 13
  for chicken, 110
  for seafood, 28, 32, 151
peanut butter
  Just Like Campfire
    S'mores, 180
  Shrimp Satay, 29
pears
  Angel Food Cake and
    Fruit Kabobs, 174
  Grilled Fruit Kabobs, 179
peas
  Asian Steak Noodle
    Salad, 36

Pea Soup with Grilled
  Hot Dogs, 33
Steak and Vegetable
  "Stir-Fry," 94
Thai Chicken Noodle
  Salad, 44
Pea Soup with Grilled Hot
  Dogs, 33
peppers, bell
  Asian Steak Noodle
    Salad, 36
  Chicken Shish Kabobs,
    23
  Crab Cakes with Red
    Pepper Aïoli, 26
  Fajitas, 98
  Grilled Cheese and
    Asparagus Rolls, 52
  Grilled Chicken
    Cacciatore, 118
  Grilled Vegetables, 48
  Hawaiian-Style Pork, 162
  Italian Vegetable and
    Orzo Salad, 42
  Lamb Kofte with
    Tzatziki, 168
  "Monterey" Cristo
    Sandwiches, 55
  Pita Fajitas, 100
  Pita Pizzas, 66
  Portobello Mushroom
    Burgers, 80
  Red Pepper Aïoli, 27
  Salami and Red Pepper
    Panini with Asiago, 60
  Sausage and Vegetable
    Herbed Pasta Toss, 164
  Steak and Vegetable
    "Stir-Fry," 94
  Tex-Mex Pasta Salad, 40
  Thai Chicken Noodle
    Salad, 44
  Veal Marsala, 170
peppers, hot
  Grilled Mango and Brie
    Quesadillas, 63
  Jalapeño Poppers, 19
  Jerk Chicken, 110
  Mexican Cheese
    Quesadillas, 64
  Mexican Steak, 103
  "Monterey" Cristo
    Sandwiches, 55
  Szechuan Chicken, 128
Pepper Steak, 102

Pesto, 117
Pesto Chicken Thighs, 116
pickerel. *See* walleye
pickles
  Creamy Turkey Burgers, 85
  Grilled Cheese Sandwich, *53*
  Tuna Melts #2, 58
Pimiento Turkey Burgers, 86
pineapple
  Angel Food Cake and Fruit Kabobs, 174
  Grilled Fruit Kabobs, 179
  Hawaiian-Style Pork, 162
  Sweet-and-Sour Sauce, 113
Pita Fajitas, 100
Pita Pizzas, 66
pork, 14. *See also* bacon; ham; sausage
  Blackened Pork Chops, 156
  Breaded Pork Chops on the Grill, 157
  Caesar burgers, *71*
  Chinese-Style Pork, 158
  curry burgers, *74*
  Hawaiian-Style Pork, 162
  Maple-Glazed Pork Chops, 159
  Mexican, *103*
  Saucy Pork Chops, 160
  Teriyaki Pork Chops, 161
  Three-Meat Panini with Provolone, 62
Portobello Mushroom Burgers, 80
Potato Pancakes, Low-Fat, 50

**Q**
quesadillas
  Chicken and Monterey Jack Quesadillas, 65
  Grilled Mango and Brie Quesadillas, 63
  Mexican Cheese Quesadillas, 64

**R**
rainbow trout
  Mustard Lemon Herb Rainbow Trout, 141

Sweet-and-Sour Rainbow Trout, 142
Red Fish, Blackened, 134
Red Pepper Aïoli, 27
red snapper, 134, 136
Reuben Sandwiches, 56
rubs
  for beef, 96, 106
  for fish, 134
  for poultry, 118, 131
rum
  Grilled Brie Pockets, 178
  Grilled Fruit Kabobs, 179

**S**
salads, 36–45
Salami and Red Pepper Panini with Asiago, 60
Salisbury Steak, Grilled, 104
salmon
  Honey Dill Salmon with Dijon, 144
  Lemon Honey Dill Salmon, 146
  Orange Soy Ginger–Glazed Salmon, 147
  Oriental Salmon Steaks, 148
  Salmon Patties, 149
Salmon Patties, 149
sandwiches, 52–66
sauces
  gravy, 104
  gremolata, 139
  Hawaiian, 162
  honey dill, 113
  Marsala, 170
  peanut, 29
  sweet-and-sour, 113
  tartar, 139
  tzatziki, 93
Saucy Pork Chops, 160
sausage
  Lentil Soup with Grilled Garlic Sausage, 34
  Maple-Glazed Sausage Sandwiches, 59
  "Monterey" Cristo Sandwiches, 55
  pea soup with, *33*
  Pita Pizzas, 66

Salami and Red Pepper Panini with Asiago, 60
Sausage and Vegetable Herbed Pasta Toss, 164
Sausage Burgers, 79
Sausage "Meatballs," 166
Three-Meat Panini with Provolone, 62
Sausage and Vegetable Herbed Pasta Toss, 164
Sausage Burgers, 79
Sausage "Meatballs," 166
Scallops, Bacon-Wrapped, 25
seafood, 14. *See also specific shellfish;* fish
Seasoned Beef Burgers, 70
sesame seeds
  Orange Soy Ginger–Glazed Salmon, 147
  Sticky Sesame Chicken, 129
shallots
  Burgers with Horseradish and Caramelized Onions, 76
  Caesar Burgers, 71
  Grilled Salisbury Steak, 104
  Wild Mushroom Bruschetta, 18
shrimp
  Chipotle Chili–Spiked Shrimp, 28
  Lemon Herb Shrimp, 150
  Lime Shrimp, Susie's, 153
  Moroccan Shrimp, 151
  Shrimp Satay, 29
  Singapore Shrimp, 152
  Tempura Shrimp and Vegetables, 30
  Thai Shrimp, 154
Shrimp Satay, 29
side dishes, 46–50
Singapore Shrimp, 152
Smoked Cheese and Turkey Breast Panini, 61
Smoky Mexican Burgers, 73

s'mores
Just Like Campfire
S'mores, 180
Tortilla S'mores, 181
snow peas
Asian Steak Noodle
Salad, 36
Steak and Vegetable
"Stir-Fry," 94
soups, 33–34
sour cream, 16
Grilled Eggplant Baba
Ghanouj, 16
Honey Dill Sauce, 113
Southern "Fried" Chicken,
111
Spicy Shrimp, 32
Steak and Vegetable
"Stir-Fry," 94
steelhead trout
honey dill with Dijon,
144
honey orange with
thyme, 145
lemon honey dill, 146
mustard lemon herb,
141
orange soy
ginger–glazed, 147
Sticky Sesame Chicken,
129
Susie's Lime Shrimp, 153
Sweet-and-Sour Rainbow
Trout, 142
Sweet-and-Sour Sauce, 113
Swiss cheese
Reuben Sandwiches, 56
Tuna Melts #1, 57
Szechuan Chicken, 128

**T**

Tarragon Mustard Chicken
Burgers, 83
Tartar Sauce, 139
Tempura Shrimp and
Vegetables, 30
Teriyaki Chicken, 130
Teriyaki Pork Chops, 161
Tex-Mex Pasta Salad, 40
Thai Chicken Noodle
Salad, 44
Thai Curry Burgers, 75
Thai Shrimp, 154
Three-Meat Panini with
Provolone, 62

Tofu, Grilled, 47
tomato
Beef Souvlaki, 92
Grilled Cheese
Sandwich, 53
Lamb Kofte with
Tzatziki, 168
Smoked Cheese and
Turkey Breast Panini,
61
Tortilla S'mores, 181
trout. *See* rainbow trout;
steelhead trout
tuna, canned
patties, 149
Tuna Melts #1, 57
Tuna Melts #2, 58
Tuna Melts #1, 57
Tuna Melts #2, 58
tuna steaks
herbed, 137
Oriental, 148
Cumin Lemon Tuna
Steaks, 143
turkey, 14
burgers with horseradish
and caramelized
onions, 76
Cheesy Turkey Burgers,
84
Creamy Turkey Burgers,
85
fajitas, 99
French Quarter burgers,
72
Green Peppercorn and
Gruyère Turkey Fillets,
131
Pimiento Turkey Burgers,
86
Smoked Cheese and
Turkey Breast Panini,
61
Thai curry burgers, 75
Turkey Mango Burgers,
87
Turkey Thyme Burgers,
88
Turkey Mango Burgers, 87
Turkey Thyme Burgers,
88
Tzatziki Sauce, 93

**U**

Ultimate Hamburger, 68

**V**

veal, 14
Chinese-Style Breaded
Veal Nuggets, 24
Italian Veal Burgers, 78
seasoned burgers, 70
Veal Marsala, 170
Veal Parmigiana, 172
Veal Marsala, 170
Veal Parmigiana, 172
vegetables. *See also specific
vegetables*
Chicken Caesar Salad, 38
Grilled Tofu, 47
Grilled Vegetables, 48
Italian Vegetable and
Orzo Salad, 42
Lentil Soup with Grilled
Garlic Sausage, 34
Low-Fat Potato
Pancakes, 50
Reuben Sandwiches, 56
Thai Chicken Noodle
Salad, 44
Tzatziki Sauce, 93

**W**

walleye
Lemon-Pepper Fish
Fillets, 138
"Pan-Fried" Grilled
Walleye, 140
Weekday Barbecued
Chicken, 109
Wild Mushroom
Bruschetta, 18
wine
Pepper Steak, 102
Sausage and Vegetable
Herbed Pasta Toss, 164
Veal Marsala, 170

**Y**

yogurt
Grilled Eggplant Baba
Ghanouj, 16
Tzatziki Sauce, 93

**Z**

zucchini
Grilled Chicken
Cacciatore, 118
Grilled Vegetables, 48
Sausage and Vegetable
Herbed Pasta Toss, 164

# More Great Books from Robert Rose

## Appliance Cooking

- 125 Best Microwave Oven Recipes
  *by Johanna Burkhard*
- 125 Best Pressure Cooker Recipes
  *by Cinda Chavich*
- The 150 Best Slow Cooker Recipes
  *by Judith Finlayson*
- Delicious & Dependable Slow Cooker Recipes
  *by Judith Finlayson*
- 125 Best Vegetarian Slow Cooker Recipes
  *by Judith Finlayson*
- America's Best Slow Cooker Recipes
  *by Donna-Marie Pye*
- Canada's Best Slow Cooker Recipes
  *by Donna-Marie Pye*
- The Best Family Slow Cooker Recipes
  *by Donna-Marie Pye*
- 125 Best Indoor Grill Recipes
  *by Ilana Simon*
- The Best Convection Oven Cookbook
  *by Linda Stephen*
- 125 Best Toaster Oven Recipes
  *by Linda Stephen*
- 250 Best American Bread Machine Baking Recipes
  *by Donna Washburn and Heather Butt*
- 250 Best Canadian Bread Machine Baking Recipes
  *by Donna Washburn and Heather Butt*

## Baking

- 250 Best Cakes & Pies
  *by Esther Brody*
- 250 Best Cobblers, Custards, Cupcakes, Bread Puddings & More
  *by Esther Brody*
- 500 Best Cookies, Bars & Squares
  *by Esther Brody*
- 500 Best Muffin Recipes
  *by Esther Brody*
- 125 Best Cheesecake Recipes
  *by George Geary*
- 125 Best Chocolate Recipes
  *by Julie Hasson*
- 125 Best Chocolate Chip Recipes
  *by Julie Hasson*
- Cake Mix Magic
  *by Jill Snider*
- Cake Mix Magic 2
  *by Jill Snider*

## Healthy Cooking

- 125 Best Vegetarian Recipes
  *by Byron Ayanoglu with contributions from Alexis Kemezys*
- The Juicing Bible
  *by Pat Crocker and Susan Eagles*
- The Smoothies Bible
  *by Pat Crocker*
- Better Baby Food
  *by Daina Kalnins, RD, CNSD and Joanne Saab, RD*
- Better Food for Kids
  *by Daina Kalnins, RD, CNSD and Joanne Saab, RD*

- 500 Best Healthy Recipes
  *Edited by Lynn Roblin, RD*
- 125 Best Gluten-Free Recipes
  *by Donna Washburn and Heather Butt*
- America's Everyday Diabetes Cookbook
  *Edited by Katherine E. Younker, MBA, RD*
- Canada's Everyday Diabetes Choice Recipes
  *Edited by Katherine E. Younker, MBA, RD*
- The Diabetes Choice Cookbook for Canadians
  *Edited by Katherine E. Younker, MBA, RD*
- The Best Diabetes Cookbook (U.S.)
  *Edited by Katherine E. Younker, MBA, RD*

## Recent Bestsellers

- 300 Best Comfort Food Recipes
  *by Johanna Burkhard*
- The Convenience Cook
  *by Judith Finlayson*
- The Spice and Herb Bible
  *by Ian Hemphill*
- 125 Best Ice Cream Recipes
  *by Marilyn Linton and Tanya Linton*
- 125 Best Casseroles & One-Pot Meals
  *by Rose Murray*
- The Cook's Essential Kitchen Dictionary
  *by Jacques Rolland*

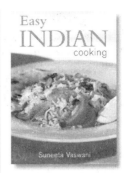

- 125 Best Ground Meat Recipes
  *by Ilana Simon*
- Easy Indian Cooking
  *by Suneeta Vaswani*
- Simply Thai Cooking
  *by Wandee Young and Byron Ayanoglu*

## Health

- The Complete Natural Medicine Guide to the 50 Most Common Medicinal Herbs
  *by Dr. Heather Boon, B.Sc.Phm., Ph.D. and Michael Smith, B.Pharm, M.R.Pharm.S., ND*
- The Complete Kid's Allergy and Asthma Guide
  *Edited by Dr. Milton Gold*
- The Complete Natural Medicine Guide to Breast Cancer
  *by Sat Dharam Kaur, ND*
- The Complete Doctor's Stress Solution
  *by Penny Kendall-Reed, MSc, ND and Dr. Stephen Reed, MD, FRCSC*
- The Complete Doctor's Healthy Back Bible
  *by Dr. Stephen Reed, MD and Penny Kendall-Reed, MSc, ND with Dr. Michael Ford, MD, FRCSC and Dr. Charles Gregory, MD, ChB, FRCP(C)*
- Everyday Risks in Pregnancy & Breastfeeding
  *by Dr. Gideon Koren, MD, FRCP(C), ND*

# Wherever books are sold

# Also Available
## from Robert Rose

125 best
ground
meat recipes

Using Beef, Turkey, Chicken, Pork and More

ILANA SIMON

**For more great books see previous pages**

Robert
**ROSE**